PROSTAMERIKA'S

RESURGENCE

How Sounders FC Roared Back to Win MLS Cup

By Steven Agen and the writers, photographers and friends of Prost Amerika

RESURGENCE

How Sounders FC Roared Back to Win MLS Cup

Copyright © 2017 PROST PUBLISHING

by Steven Agen

ISBN-13: 978-0999216408
ISBN-10: 0999216408

PROSTPUBLISHING
www.prostamerika.com/books
Email: info@prostpublishing.com

Contents

Foreword by "Mr. Sounder" Zach Scott

Preface by Steve Clare, founder of Prost Amerika and Prost Publishing

Foreword
Aloha and Goodbye

By Zach Scott

Zach Scott joined Sounders in 2002 and by the time of his retirement had made 289 appearances.
Such was the loyalty of this one-club man that he was given the honor "Mr. Sounder."

It is safe to say that there was no better way to end my career than winning MLS Cup. It was the culmination of years of hard training, hours of marking some excellent opponents, and the joy and honor of playing alongside some amazing players and fantastic human beings.

A certain amount of sacrifice is always necessary in sports and most of it came from my wife, Alana and my kids, Kalei, Ka'ena, and Lina. I'd be remiss to not thank them for their unwavering support, my fondest memories are of meeting them on the pitch after a win to kick the ball around as a family.

Anyone who has followed my career knows that I've had to work hard and few things came easily at the start of my life. Finding soccer teams to play with, never mind against, was tough in Hawaii in the 1980s. I could not have wished for a more supportive individual than my mom Linda who would drive me and my brother Daniel all over Maui to find soccer.

She shaped me in another way. She never told us we had played well when we hadn't. It was the era of "in soccer everybody wins," but not in our house. Honesty was the key to improvement and I like to think I was always well aware of what needed improvement in my game right up until the end.

I tried to be honest on the pitch and give everything I had for my teammates, my coaches and especially the fans. Defending has its tricky nuances and of course I employed every trick, dirty or clean, but always in the knowledge that my forward teammates were also having them used against us.

This led to some funny moments. Once when I went forward for a corner at an Open Cup tie, I felt a defender give me a rough shove in the back. I turned round on instinct to intimidate him, only to see the face of my brother Daniel cracking himself up with laughter. I got the last laugh that day as we beat Kitsap 2-1 and went on to win the Open Cup, a tournament that has always had a special place in my heart.

But if we're talking about special places in my heart, then Seattle, the Emerald City, has to be at the top. I arrived in 1998 to attend Gonzaga and 19 years later I'm still here, certainly a one-club man but also a one-city man.

Let's not forget soccer is also a passion of mine. Internationally Arsenal became my English team. That year, 1998, my arrival at Gonzaga did not quite make as many headlines as the world famous Swedish international Freddie Ljungberg joining Arsenal at roughly the same time. If you'd told me that at the time, 11 years later we'd be teammates, I'd have thought you were crazy.

MLS, Adrian Hanauer, Joe Roth and Sigi Schmid made that happen. I like to think that between us, Freddie and I, could do all aspects of the beautiful game, but I was the better man-marker and astonishingly got on better with referees!

My post-soccer career has taken me away from the sport but being invited to write the Foreword to a book celebrating our MLS Cup win is a nice honor. Prost Amerika has been covering my career and the Seattle Sounders since the USL days, good ones and bad ones, and they know as well as any outlet the ups and downs of my career, from forming that hard man defence with Danny Jackson and Taylor Graham to looking down the line-up at anthem time and seeing Ljungberg, Clint Dempsey or Osvaldo Alonso.

Lastly, I want to thank the fans. I attended a match this season as a fan for the first time and still saw replica jerseys with "Scott" on the back. Pretty cool for a boy from Maui to see.

This Foreword gives me one last chance to say:

Thank you Seattle. Thank you Sounders.

Zach Scott looking back on a successful career
Photo by Matt Warso

Preface
The Editor's Notes

By Steve Clare

Steve Clare is the founder of Prost Amerika and Prost Publishing.

It's been a decade since Prost Amerika first started covering Seattle Sounders. Then, it was USL rather than MLS. Many other things haven't changed. In those days Adrian Hanauer was Majority Owner, Brian Schmetzer was the head coach and the team played both at Qwest Field and Starfire.

They were also winners then – and now. In 2007, the club won the national title and by 2016, that was to be repeated. In between there were Open Cups, a Supporters Shield and Cascadia Cups. Zach Scott was around then and stayed long enough to see his team win MLS Cup and of course write the Foreword to this book. Other figures such as Bart Wiley and Taylor Graham have also been consistent presences.

But all of us have seen changes that override the constant presences. I could talk about the rise in attendances, or the amount of money circulating in the soccer economy, the standard of global star who plays and the harder to measure changed level of consciousness of the soccer team in the city, the tremendous community involvement the supporter culture brings. All have changed immensely in our ten years of reporting on Sounders FC.

After 10 years covering the club, it is an honour and delight to be publishing a book about an MLS Cup win. It's an even bigger honour to include the cream of Seattle soccer journalists; Art Thiel, Matt Pentz, Steven Agen, Andrew Harvey as well as America's best match announcer Richard Fleming who brings a view from outside Seattle, and the Mayor who brought MLS to Seattle Greg Nickels as well as our beat writers, Toby Dunkelberg and Ed Pham.

At Prost, we are very proud of our photographers. We have a legion of them around MLS and that enabled us to select the best shots from Sounders season home and away.

When you go into a bookshop, there is now regularly a soccer section. That is an improvement on ten years ago. Still however, less than half those books are about Americans and American soccer. We are on a mission to change that. It may take another ten years, but we'll gladly be there every step of the way. Books are important. No sub-culture can exist without a body of literature for the kind of in-depth and evergreen writing that the speed of the web cannot sustain. Books can inspire a child's unique ability for imagination.

Seattle Sounders are no strangers to titles
Photo by Nick Danielson

I'd like to end by thanking all those involved in bringing this book to fruition and of course all those who have covered soccer for Prost Amerika, in Seattle and beyond.

Chapter One
The Road Less Traveled

By Former Seattle Mayor, Gregory Nickels

Greg Nickels was the 51st mayor of Seattle and held office from January 1, 2002 – January 1, 2010.

I am a Seattle guy, but it wasn't always so. My grandparents were born in Chicago in the 1890's. My father was born in Chicago in 1925 and followed by me 30 years later. That is to say, in sporting terms, I was born a Cubs fan. That was the way it was. There was no soccer equivalent in the United States. Certainly soccer existed. In fact just two years before my birth a Chicago-based team won the US Open Cup. But Falcons FC couldn't hold a candle to the Cubs.

Somewhere along the way I learned to love Seattle and the beautiful game. Oh, and politics (but that's for a different story)!

It might have been my dad taking us kids to Lower Woodland in the early 60's to watch the area's highest-level amateur soccer on Sunday afternoons. The Seattle Hungarians were the team to beat in those days, though there was also a very good team comprised of Scandinavians as I recall. Now I have no idea why Dad took us to these matches. He had not played or seen soccer growing up as far as I know. Perhaps it was to give Mom some respite, or maybe because it was free.

In those days, soccer was played in Seattle's Catholic schools, and I got to play for the school team from Our Lady of Guadalupe in West Seattle. I was a couple of years behind Ballan Campeau (later a Sounder goalkeeper) and a couple years ahead of Jimmy McAlister (later a Sounders winger). When we moved to Capitol Hill before seventh grade, I joined the mighty St. Joe's program and was relegated to the second team.

The (Bon) Fire is Lit

Those experiences must have lit a pilot light in me because a few years later I had the chance to go in on Sounders season tickets with my Dad and I jumped at it. It was the first adult thing my Dad and I did together and made me feel very grown up. While the first two years the Sounders NASL team played in Memorial Stadium, they soon moved to the ultra-modern Kingdome. In fact on

Nickels moved the legislation to create the new stadium
Photo by Nick Danielson

April 25, 1976 over 58,000 of us watched the Seattle Sounders and the New York Cosmos play in the first sports event held in that futuristic facility.

'Turf' back then meant AstroTurf, effectively a thin layer of indoor-outdoor carpeting laid over asphalt. Boy did the ball bounce! But we didn't care, we didn't know any better. And we were treated to some decent soccer played by young Americans like Campeau, McAlister and Jeff Stock; lovable long-in-the-tooth EPL (then called English 1st Division) footballers such as Englishman Alan Hinton, Wales' Mike England and proud Scot Jimmy Gabriel and opposing team's exotic world stars including Pele and Franz Beckenbauer. My favorite games were against the Vancouver Whitecaps. Many hundreds of their fans would trek to Seattle and were easily spotted by the distinctive white caps they wore.

It was with great sadness that Dad and I watched the NASL Sounders fold in September 1983 with the league following suit 18-months later.

In 1987 I was elected to the King County Council. I was now, in effect, one of the landlords of the Kingdome! No one who watched the soccer ball bounce in the Kingdome in those early days or came indoors on a sunny Seattle day to watch baseball really believed that facility was the best we could do. But it had opened the door. And I could now influence events.

A couple of years later the Mariners were threatening to move to Tampa Bay. Believing that if I were to play a part in keeping baseball in Seattle I needed to put my money where my mouth was, I became a Mariners season ticket holder and remained one for twenty years. I was the prime sponsor of the legislation creating the ballpark public authority and imposing the taxes to pay for a new home for baseball. My political career and my sporting passion had met. They were to never be parted.

To be honest I was less sanguine about the need for a new home for American football. With ten home games during our wet season an indoor facility seemed to work well and for those of an outdoor bent there were the University of Washington Huskies a couple of miles north. But as the public endorsed the idea in a statewide referendum in June 1997, I began to warm up to the idea. And as it became clear this opened the door to a future soccer franchise (MLS had begun play just a year earlier), I became a proponent and helped move the necessary legislation along to allow for the replacement of the Kingdome with a new soccer/football stadium.

When the new 'Seahawks Stadium' opened in 2002, the first sporting event was, in fact, soccer. It seemed as though Seattle had graduated to the big leagues.

And so it was with great anticipation that, six months to the day following my Dad's passing in May 2007, the announcement of an MLS franchise for Seattle was received in our household. Two weeks later my wife Sharon and I were season ticket holders; in part to honor Dad's love of the sport but largely to satisfy my own passion and share it with my own family as he had with me.

By the time the 2009 inaugural season finally came, it was clear things had changed from my experience thirty years earlier. Supporters groups did not exist in the NASL days, though there was a Sounder Booster club. The league had grown well beyond the earlier core of older British players, though thanks to David Beckham that demographic was not excluded. We were still playing on 'turf' but it wasn't the same stuff that destroyed Ken Griffey's legs. And we were playing outdoors. In March and April it wasn't clear this was a good thing but come June, July and August, it would be glorious.

While I consider myself an average fan, I was Mayor during the inaugural season and got the rare privilege of joining the new franchise's owners on opening day to kick off the first 'March to the Match' from Occidental Park in Pioneer Square to the 'Xbox 360 Pitch.'

Then it was off to check out our seats in the 'All-Inclusive North End' section. All-Inclusive meant access to the concession food was included in the ticket price (for a couple bucks more). It turned out to be a terrible choice. The food was awful and unhealthy. The seats may have been uncomfortable as well, I don't really know. We stood for the National Anthem and didn't sit again for 45 minutes – which also was new.

The experience taught me that when it comes to soccer, being a fan beats being a 'dignitary' by a mile.

Expectations were high prior to the season. Some 22,000 season tickets had been sold. The previous year's MLS Cup-winning coach had been hired to manage the club and a Swedish underwear modeling Premier League winger was signed as a Designated Player (DP). Opening Day did not disappoint as 32,523 fans watched the Sounders shut out the New York Red Bulls 3– 0.

In fact we became the first MLS expansion side to win our first three matches – and all by shutout. I remember well our first loss, against the Wizards of Kansas City. Our goalkeeper and Sounders legend Kasey Keller left with a red card for handling the ball outside the 18-yard box. I can still picture the moment even though I listened to the game on the radio because I had given my tickets to my son.

There were many great moments that first season; Seattle became the second expansion side (the Chicago Fire were the first) to make the playoffs in its first season. There was that Open Cup victory in DC. The team set a league attendance record with an average of 30,897 fans per match! That was 10,070 per game more than

the second placed team, the LA Galaxy and more than San Jose, Kansas City and Dallas combined!

It felt like the new MLS Sounders and Seattle were meant for one another.

The second season, 2010, saw an increase to 32,000 season ticket holders. The team again broke the league attendance record drawing 36,173 per match. We repeated the US Open Cup triumph and competed in the CONCACAF Champions League for the first time. And for the second straight year, the team made the playoffs, again to be dispatched early.

Sharon and I moved from the All-Inclusive North to seats adjacent to the Emerald City Supporters in the Brougham (South) End. We loved our new seats next to the ECS, there so much energy packed into those three General Admission sections! It was also a chance to observe 'supporter' culture vs. 'fan' culture and see the potential for conflict where the two intersected.

The following season, 2011, the team once again set a league attendance record. The Sounders won the US Open Cup for the third year running in front of 35,615 home fans – a record that still stands for a USOC Final. We were the first team to win three straight USOC titles since the Greek American SC of New York City in the late 1960's.

The high-point for a veteran like me was seeing two Cascadia rivals from the old NASL days join the Sounders in MLS. The addition of Portland (the one in Oregon) and Vancouver (the one in British Columbia) would add spice that could only be faintly rivaled by beating LA Galaxy in Carson. To top it off the revered Cascadia Cup would again feature all three ancient rivals and Sounders FC claimed it.

The Sounders three-year US Open Cup run ended in 2012 on a controversial shootout defeat in the Cup Final to the newly-rebranded Sporting Kansas City. The referee, Ricardo Salazar, has still not been forgiven by Sounders faithful for some of his calls in that one. The team again led the league in attendance and again made the playoffs but with a positive twist – they finally won a playoff series before being booted in the Western Conference Championships by the Galaxy, the eventual Cup winners.

In 2013 the Sounders rocked MLS by signing USMNT Captain Clint Dempsey to a multiyear deal. The highly produced announcement of this deal was made before a Sounders home match and set the crowd on fire. It was about this time I subscribed to MLS Live, a subscription service that allows access to out of market MLS games throughout the season. I've enjoyed watching our Cascadia and Western Conference rivals week in and week out and learning about this league. I've gone from Seattle dignitary to MLS diehard on my own personal journey.

Once more the club set a new attendance record (over 44,000) and once again underperformed in the playoffs, winning the knock-out game but falling to Portland in the next round.

But a new triumph was on its way. Sounders won their first Supporters Shield as the best team in the regular season. They also returned to glory in the US Open Cup winning their fourth title in their short MLS history.

Still MLS Cup glory proved elusive, and I guess you could say it was around that time that expectations finally overtook reality.

With even these two trophies in hand they failed to advance to MLS Cup, losing to nemesis LA Galaxy on away goals in the Western Conference Championships (after having defeated FC Dallas on away goals in the previous round). At the end of the season the team sold its most promising young star DeAndre Yedlin to the English Premier League.

It all had been such fun plain sailing for those opening five years but now a rockier patch awaited.

Toward the end of the 2014 campaign, I had noticed a couple of things of concern. There were increasingly physical confrontations between fans and supporters near our section. This was not helped by fans being loudly exhorted to move if they didn't like having their views blocked by frequent flag waving. Although we were never directly involved, the prudent and fair thing seemed to be to move rather than prevent those most passionate of supporters from doing their thing. We found other seats and I'm glad to say the supporters are still bringing it every home game.

Opening week of the 2015 season saw Orlando City draw 62,000 to their inaugural match, sending a shot across the Sounders bow. Our stranglehold on topping the league in attendance was loosening just a bit. Expectations for the Sounders, always high, hit stratospheric levels entering the 2015 season. And for the first few weeks of the young season the Sounders were meeting the unrealistically high expectations and through June were leading the Western Conference.

Then something completely shook the very firmaments of Sounder culture. Called the Red Card Wedding, it was an US Open Cup match between the Sounders and the Portland Timbers on June 16th at the team's Starfire training-facility stadium. Sounders fans were pretty confident going in. This was our tournament, no one owned the USOC like the Sounders had in the MLS-era. The Timbers hated Starfire because they had never won there. I do not recall if there was a full moon, but certainly there was some mischief afoot.

The Timbers won the match but that is only part of a sortied episode. The Sounders wonderful striker, Obafemi Martins suffered an injury that ended his game and kept him out of action for several weeks. Since the team had already used their three substitutions, this left them playing with ten men. Then team leader Clint Dempsey, apparently frustrated with the inexperienced referee grabbed his referee's notebook and tore it to shreds (leading to a long USOC suspension and a shorter MLS sanction). This was stunning, to say the least and got him a red card. There were two additional red cards given to Sounders players and at the end they had only seven players on the field.

The night changed the course of Sounders season. The loss of Martins (groin injury) and Dempsey (suspension and Gold Cup duty) led to a summer-long spiral for the team.

This was particularly unfortunate for us in that I had just decided to attend my first out-of-town Sounders match against the lowly Chicago Fire. I was able to convince twenty or so of my hockey-loving Chicago cousins to join Sharon and me at a soccer match. Alas our diminished Sounders saw the lowly Fire win 1-0 with a goal at the death.

A late season rally saw us back into the playoffs and a nice surprise – we finally beat the LA Galaxy in a playoff round. Unfortunately, we then fell to FC Dallas on penalty kicks.

Then, after we were eliminated, came perhaps the lowest point of our Sounders history ... the MLS Cup was claimed by the Portland Timbers. The upstart Timbers, not the Sounders, were the first Cascadia team to win the ultimate MLS prize. It was unthinkable and absurd yet there it was. I suppose worse things have happened but at the time it was hard to imagine what. It has always been expected, perhaps even accepted, that Sounders would be the first side from Cascadia to hoist the Cup.

I think it would be fair to say that it rocked our perceptions of where we stood. Still angry going into the 2016 season, the Sounders early season performance got me asking questions I had never considered – maybe we weren't that good, maybe we were a mediocre team destined to troll the lower levels of our domestic league.

Two important team offensive cogs were sent packing, Lamar Neagle to DC United and Marco Pappa to Colorado Rapids, leaving the team shorthanded if Clint Dempsey or rookie Jordan Morris were called away or hurt. We lost Obafemi Martins when the team chose to sell his rights to a Chinese-league team that apparently was willing to pay him much more than his signed Seattle contract.

During the first half of the season the team that had raised expectations time and again, had done the impossible were, in a word, terrible. At times unwatchable. They were buried near the bottom of the table and there were no longer any expectations to be met. In one final blow, star forward Clint Dempsey was forced out of play, and perhaps out of his soccer career, with an irregular heartbeat. Our season seemed done.

And then on July 24th, the team let go of the only coach in their MLS history and replaced him with his assistant, Brian Schmetzer. The same day the team announced the signing of Nicolas Lodeiro as a DP. The team that had such high expectations throughout its MLS history waited until there were virtually no expectations, until they were all but eliminated from contention to make an improbable, heroic run to greatness.

And that, as they say, made all the difference.

The rest of the season's story is covered in the rest of the book. I will read it with glee.

Did I ever see it coming when I sat in my first Council meeting talking about sports stadia?

Not really, but even politicians have dreams; especially when they are and have always been soccer fans first.

ECS bring out their inner Rick Astley
Photo by Nick Danielson

Chapter Two
The Preseason View

By Steven Agen

Steven Agen is the Seattle Editor for Prost Amerika and founder of Radio Cascadia.

2015 — Self-inflicted injury to which insult is added

The Seattle Sounders entered their 2016 campaign on the heels of perhaps their most tumultuous season ever the year before.

Clint Dempsey and Obafemi Martins had picked up where they left off in 2014, Sounders' most successful year in MLS to date at the time. That season, the two had combined down the center to astonishing results and ultimately two of American soccer's three major trophies. Through nine league matches in 2015, they tallied thirteen goals between them. For a moment, many around the country thought perhaps Seattle would be the class of the league until one of Dempsey or Martins left or got too old to perform well. After averaging more than 1.8 points per game in their previous 43 league matches, it wasn't hard to see why.

Seattle's prolific strike force had them at the top of the standings in June again, and they seemed to be waltzing to a second-consecutive Supporters' Shield. The season was thrown into upheaval thanks to an infamous Open Cup match with archrivals Portland.

Red Card Wedding

Brad Evans was dismissed on 69 minutes and then Martins went down with an injury just after tying the match at one with just more than ten minutes to play. The referee blew his whistle to conclude regular time, and Sounders would have to survive an eleven-on-nine situation for a full half an hour.

Portland regained the lead on one hundred minutes even but the terrible night still wasn't over yet for Seattle. Michael Azira was the next Sounder to leave the pitch early after his forceful studs-up challenge saw him red carded on 113' and, as fans pondered what an eight-on-eleven soccer match would look like, Clint Dempsey stole the show, or at least the referee's card.

Dempsey snatched Daniel Radford's red card away from him and proceeded to tear it up. That naturally earned the former USA captain his own sending-off, and eventually a 6 match ban from the Open Cup. Dempsey's petulant action was the capper on a wildly undisciplined evening from Sigi Schmid's charges. Portland would go on to add a third goal while enjoying their four-man advantage, and Seattle's unbeaten record in Open Cup at their Tukwila-based

Oba Martins left days before the start of the 2016 season
Photo by Lyndsay Radnedge

second home was finally over after nine years, two leagues and 22 matches.

The Aftermath

The match captured the attention of all of American soccer – it had everything, rivalry, goals, red cards and cup football – and was soon dubbed the 'Red Card Wedding.'

If failing their Open Cup title defense at the first hurdle wasn't a big enough blow, the injury Obafemi Martins sustained during the match was plenty to derail Sounders' spotless league campaign as well. After only losing three times in their first fifteen matches, Seattle lost nine of their next eleven games in a truly disastrous summer. Martins finally returned to the side in August, two months removed from the injury at Starfire.

The match had taken more than just Martins from Sounders, though, and they never hit their stride again in late 2015 the way they did in the first several months of the season.

Roman Torres, Erik Friberg, Nelson Valdez and Andreas Ivanschitz all arrived via transfer as the club pressed the panic button in August. The Front Office certainly came back from their historically-poor summer, posting two months' worth of unbeaten results heading into the playoffs, but it just wasn't the same. Sounders weren't dominating their opponents the way the same lineup had in March through June. With all four players already on the wrong side of thirty years of age, and specifically with Torres going down with a torn ACL at San Jose in early September, Sounders' core of veterans were physically worn down by the time the playoffs rolled around. Their fourth place finish was the most fans could hope for after their prior struggles.

A 3-2 win in the Western Conference Knockout Round set up a date with first-place Dallas. The writing was on the wall as Seattle's older

Brad Evans began to gel with Chad Marshall in defense
Photo by Matt Warso

roster sputtered in their second match in four days, the first leg of the Conference Semifinals played at CenturyLink Field. Fabian Castillo grabbed a vital away goal for the visitors before Sounders pulled a rabbit out of the hat and stormed back to win 2-1 on the night. The question was, would they have the legs for the return match?

The answer was a resounding "no." At full time the series sat at 3-3, and extra time followed. Dempsey and Martins, practically unplayable by defenses earlier in the season, failed to generate a single chance in the additional half hour after being placed on an island for the first ninety minutes. A penalty shootout defeat was next for them after two of Seattle's first three takers missed their spot kicks.

The club was left to wonder how the situation they found themselves in on the morning of June 13, the Red Card Wedding, devolved into the one they found themselves in the day of the Dallas exit.

In 2014 and early 2015, it felt like the club had finally began firing on all cylinders for the first time in their MLS history. As their attention turned to 2016, finding a way to replicate the form of that incredible 43-game stretch was of paramount importance.

Portland Wins MLS Cup

If watching complete control of a league slip through their hands was the injury, seeing Portland win MLS Cup in November, 2015 was the insult. Timbers downed a slate of Western Conference opponents on the road, including FC Dallas, before completing the rare feat of winning the cup on the road as well.

After Portland failed to win a major trophy for their first forty years of existence, taking the trophy that Sounders coveted above all else threw a new sting in the rivalry. More importantly for Seattle's 2016

season, it lit a fire under both the front office and fanbase. The heat had many predicting a big offseason for Seattle, replete with signings and renewed vigor.

As time would come to tell, the road wouldn't be that smooth or simple for Seattle.

Preseason Camp 2016

Departures of key veterans who helped Sounders peak in 2014, like Marco Pappa and Lamar Neagle, opened up a sizable chunk of salary cap space for new signings. Most of the rumors surrounding potential acquisitions focused on Mercer Island native Jordan Morris, the HomeGrown-eligible Stanford super-prospect with offers on the table in Germany's top flight.

By January, it became clear that Seattle intended to utilize the SuperDraft to fill a number of vacancies on the roster. A successful day saw Sounders trade down and still select their favorite center back from the year's recruits.

Joevin Jones, a 24 year old Trinidadian left back who played the 2015 season in Chicago, also moved over on draft day. Sounders General Manager Garth Lagerwey spoke to local media via teleconference after the conclusion of the first several rounds and immediately had important and kind words for the defender. Despite not yet being officially identified in the trade that sent him to Seattle, Lagerwey spoke highly of their player-to-be-named, "We feel we picked up a starter for our team today."

Morris had announced his decision to forego his senior year at Stanford ten days before the draft, and a day after he officially put pen to paper with Seattle. The deal was the biggest in the history of the MLS HomeGrown Player program, worth more than $600,000 in his first season, After years of keeping the US Men's National Team waiting, telling VfL Wolfsburg that they'd missed out on his

services was just the latest example of Morris sticking religiously to his own path.

As February rolled around, Seattle began to prepare for their tie with Club America in the quarterfinals of the CONCACAF Champions League. Their focus on the regional power was severely disrupted by reports out of Asia linking Obafemi Martins to Shanghai Shenhua of the Chinese Super League.

Martins was always known as a mercenary during his European career. After staying with Inter Milan for five seasons between 2001 and 2006, he never stayed at a club for more than three years. After three seasons in Seattle and 83 total appearances, the most outside of his 136 for Inter and 104 for Newcastle United, the striker had stuck around in the Pacific Northwest for far longer than most had expected.

With that in mind, it was fair for the Nigerian to ask the club to allow him to move on to his next adventure. Adrian Hanauer, Lagerwey and their staff have never been ones to hold players back from their dreams, and this was no exception. Without even a publicly-touted counteroffer to match his similar new salary in China (notably not affected by double taxation, as Martins' pay was in Seattle), Sounders let perhaps their most dynamic player ever leave.

Between the much-hyped addition of Morris and the fact that Sounders were previously carrying three Designated Player forwards, allowing Martins to leave made competitive sense on a surface level.

However, Martins officially signed for Shanghai Shenhua on February 18th — exactly five days before Seattle's first leg fixture with Club America. Fan perception on the tie went from hopeful to negative. In fact, the focus switched from the club's continental chances to how long it would taker for Morris to settle in as Martins' successor.

Martins had tallied 43 goals in his 83 appearances for Seattle. It marked by far the most prolific clip an MLS-era Sounder has scored at, and he was surely on target to break Fredy Montero's all-time club record of 60 goals (accomplished in four years and 160 appearances). His departure rocked a Seattle offseason that, on the whole, featured few other big shake ups. Unfortunately for Sounders, this shake up came at such a vital time that it would reverberate through the first several months of the MLS season as well. Champions League progression was almost out of the question without him.

pg 26: The Tunnel
Photo by Max Aquino

pg 27: Clint Dempsey up close
Photo by Brandon Bleek

Chapter Three

Treading Water
The First Nine Games

By Toby Dunkelberg

Toby Dunkelberg covers Sounders FC for Prost Amerika.

Champions League

By advancing from their group in 2015, Sounders moved on to the knockout round of the 2015-16 CONCACAF Champions League. Their quarterfinal matchup would be a home and home with Club America of Mexico. It was a difficult draw for the Sounders as Club America is one of the biggest and best clubs in all of North America. It was to be an uphill battle from the start as only two MLS sides had ever advanced past a Mexican team in the knockout round of the tournament. Fortunately, the Sounders happened to be one of them.

The nine days went by quickly as Sigi Schmid tried to get his side ready for the match. Liga MX sides play a summer and a winter season. As a result, Club America was in full fitness as their season had been underway for months. Seattle on the other hand still had players getting into full fitness as they were still in the midst of their normal MLS preseason.

The first game ended in a 2-2 draw after the Sounders twice saw themselves go up a goal only to surrender the equalizers shortly after. While Seattle held their own, it became immediately apparent that Club America's attack was dangerous. They took advantage of all of Seattle's mistakes turning a little bit of space and a slightly loose mark into a goal.

The bright spot for the Sounders was that they managed to score twice despite the lack of Obafemi Martins. They flew south knowing that they could play at America's level. They also knew that they needed to win at the Cathedral of Mexican Futbol, Estadio Azteca, where no American team had ever won before.

Everything went according to plan for 41 glorious minutes. Seattle remained sound in the back. Snuffing out chances any way that they could, hoping that they could somehow get a goal and defend it.

Then in the 41st minute that dream came true. Nelson Valdez and Pablo Aguilar both went for an Osvaldo Alonso cross and in the commotion it slipped off of Aguilar and into America's goal.

Seattle was up 1-0 in the match and 3-2 on aggregate. They were 49 minutes away from becoming the first American club side to win at the Vahalla of Mexican sport.

Club America's attack was dangerous
Photo by Max Aquino

The Sounders hopes were dashed just a minute later when Rubens Sambueza launched a cross to Carlos Quintero who directed it past Frei. Oribe Peralta sealed the deal four minutes later with another goal.

From then on it was the Club America show. They scored again in the second half and continued to generate chances. With a final score of 3-1, and 5-3 on aggregate, Sounders FC found itself eliminated from the 2015-2016 CONCACAF Champions League.

Club America went on to win the tournament, and the Sounders played well against them, but it was little consolation. Seattle prides itself on always striving to be better and winning the Champions League is a longtime goal for the entire organization, and MLS as a whole. They'd have to have quick memories though. The MLS season was just three days away.

MLS – Sounders suffer three starting losses

The first MLS match of the season is a time of hope for all clubs. But the league's legendary parity means that no one knows for sure what's in store for the rest of the year. The season could end short of the playoffs in October. Or, great play, depth, and a lot of luck could see your team playing in a one-off match in December with the MLS Cup on the line.

Sounders fans have come to expect a lot of their franchise. The organization had never missed a playoff in its MLS history. While the Martins departure dampened expectations, this was a team just a couple months removed from being penalty kicks away from advancing to the Western Conference Finals. More recently they'd held a lead over club America three times in a home-and-home series.

And yet for all the positives there were still many unknowns. How would Jordan Morris adapt to MLS? Could Joevin Jones or Dylan Remick step up to the everyday left back job? And most

importantly, how would Seattle score without the Dempsey-Martins partnership?

As the fireworks of the season opening ceremony faded into the rain pouring down onto the Xbox Pitch, answers began to come to the surface. Joevin Jones got the start with Oniel Fisher on the right for an injured Tyrone Mears. The play against Sporting Kansas City was ugly, and it was a physical battle the entire 90.

Despite that, Seattle's offense showed signs of life. Chad Marshall reasserted his aerial dominance when he rose for a header that clattered off the bar on a corner from Ivanschitz. Morris ended up with a sterling one-on- one chance on a ball in behind but the rookie couldn't slip it past the keeper. Clint Dempsey followed that up by narrowly missing grabbing a goal off a free kick. Three big distinct cogs in the Sounders attack were goal dangerous.

Things changed in the 41st minute when the Sounders went down to 10 men after a brash tackle from Fisher earned him a red card. After that, it was SKC's game. The Sounders had one more chance but in the end the lack of a man proved too much and SKC managed to snag a goal in the 73rd minute off a fluke shot from distance that Stefan Frei flubbed.

A red card loss is always taken with a grain of salt, especially one as close as the game against SKC, so hopes were still high.

A week later the team traveled to Sandy, Utah to take on Real Salt Lake. Frei was a late scratch from goal meaning Tyler Miller got the start. On a brighter note, Mears was back and fully healthy. The Sounders kicked things off with a beautiful team goal that Alonso finished. But just like against SKC, defensive miscues at the back cost Seattle the game. RSL beat Miller with a snap header and when the challenged him on a ball he should've punched away.

Once again judgement was reserved. RSL's a tough place to play and Miller made rookie mistakes that cost them a result. The lost to Vancouver was much the same. Two questionable PK's by Fisher and Marshall gifted the Whitecaps two goals and the Sounders couldn't find the equalizer after a beautiful free kick from Ivanschitz fooled 'Caps keeper David Ousted.

Now at three loses in their first three games — a first for the MLS Sounders – concern started to grow. The attack was failing to gel, the defense was more porous than hoped and Seattle sat at the very bottom of the table with zero points.

Things starting to gel

A 1-0 home win against Montreal did little to silence to first two concerns but the three points earned by Dempsey's 79th minute header were welcomed nonetheless.

The shutout was the biggest takeaway as it was the first time the ideal backline and keeper started together. Marshall and Evans manned the center, and the hope grew that the defense could cover while the Sounders got over their injury bug and Morris began to harmonize his effort with that of Dempsey and Valdez.

It came together down in Houston a week later. Morris was back after missing the Montreal game but Aaron Kovar was in for Valdez who had picked up a knock. Houston went up in the first half off a fantastic bit of finesse from Sounders' perennial worst nightmare Giles Barnes. The offense struggled to break down a Houston defense that was content with the 1-0 score line. The Sounders managed to come away with a result thanks to Marshall's goal off an Oalex Anderson cross in the last minute of stoppage.

Anderson was Sigi Schmid's most attacking option off the bench and the assist was a nice feather in his cap after being brought in four of the first five games.

A week later against Philadelphia in Seattle, the rookie got his first MLS start. Nelson Valdez was still out and the youngster had impressed off the bench and fit perfectly into Sigi Schmid's 4-3-3 that he was still trying to make work.

The Sounders dominated the Union in the first half, generating chances but once again failing to convert. It took another set piece goal from Chad Marshall for the Sounders to get their first tally.

Then Ivanschitz made a perfect pass over the top to Jordan Morris. The rookie with all the hype had done everything. He had been making the runs, getting the chances and even combining well with Dempsey. He just couldn't get direct the ball on target. But in front of the 39,620 Morris finally put it together. He quick timed it and tapped the ball by Union keeper Andre Blake for his first professional goal. Philadelphia scored two minutes later but the game was over, and Morris was ready to go.

With Dempsey and Valdez out against Colorado, Morris had to be ready because like it or not he was the most experienced and goal dangerous player Seattle had. Just like before, Morris did everything right. Having gotten over the psychological hump of scoring his first goal, he was on target again quickly, this time in the 41st minute. His effort tied the game, after Colorado had grabbed an early lead. But the combination of Colorado's physicality and the lack of offensive threats other than Morris did the Sounders in as they fell 3-1 in Colorado.

Dempsey returned from injury and Joevin Jones once again got the start at left back over Dylan Remick. When Jones was in, he'd done well getting forward and had shown a knack for getting past defenders to launch off crosses. But he'd also been caught out of position in addition to being loose on his marks.

His crossing prowess was on display again against Columbus Crew on April 30th. Jones also did a much better job of timing his runs forward. The game remained deadlocked at zero until the 88th minute when Morris once again came through in a big way. He got on the end of a rebound from Jones and Anderson to get the game winner and make it three straight games with a goal scored.

Up next was San Jose. The Quakes had been Seattle's bogie team. Over the years, it had frequently seemed as if whenever Seattle has been shorthanded due to suspensions, injuries or call ups, the Earthquakes were the opponent. So there was a bit of apprehension going into the match. The lineup announcement of Kovar, Morris, and Herculez Gomez up top only made matters worse. Even with Dempsey sitting behind them, there was genuine concern that they wouldn't be up to the task.

They put those to rest within the first 30 minutes. A great sequence of passing found Clint Dempsey wide open in the box. The long time USMNT forward made no mistake about it to put Seattle up 1-0. A very back and forth game saw Frei come off his line twice to make a save in addition to the Quakes' free kick that clattered off the crossbar.

Then in the 84th minute it looked like San Jose was about to steal away another result. Tyrone Mears went to ground to pull Quakes center back Victor Bernardez down for the penalty. Chris Wondolowski stepped up to take it and to the surprise of everyone at CenturyLink Field, he bounced it off the post. Then, to add a cherry on top, in the 89th minute Morris took a crack at goal from distance that eluded David Bingham. The strike gave him a goal in four consecutive matches and ensured Sounders would take all three points on the night.

The win over San Jose made for their fourth straight home win. Seattle had fully responded from their initial three loses. Since then they'd gone 4-1-1 and had catapulted themselves back into playoff contention. They were also looking like one of the hottest teams in the West. Having weathered injuries to key players, and the lose of

Obafemi Martins, they had still come out in the middle of the pack. And with Jones and Morris growing into real contributors there was real hope in Seattle.

But lurking under the surface was a team that hadn't scored more than two goals in a game, and had serious depth issues in the attack. And those issues were about to be brought kicking and screaming into the light.

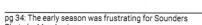

pg 34: The early season was frustrating for Sounders
Photo by Max Aquino

pg 35: Jordan Morris causes problems for the Quakes
Photo by Nick Danielson

THE SEATTLE SPORTS BAR IN SAN DIEGO

"SAN DIEGO'S BEST DRAFT SELECTION & ROTATION"
- WEST COASTER MAGAZINE 2016

THEBREWPROJECT.COM

Chapter Four

How Sounders Were Born, and Seahawks Saved

By Art Thiel

Art Thiel is a longtime Seattle sports columnist and co-founder of Sportspress Northwest (sportspressnw.com).

Youngsters and newbies to the Seattle-area marketplace may be under the impression that the original story of the Sounders championship began shortly before the inaugural 2009 expansion season. That would miss the truth by about a dozen years.

MLS Sounders may not be in existence, and certainly would not be flourishing, without a seminal event that took place on June 17, 1997. A successful special election in Washington State – the only measure on the the ballot – seeded the Sounders and saved the NFL Seahawks, both of which responded by returning championships to the state while becoming two of the most formidable franchises in North American sports.

A paper-thin majority of voters said yes to a set of user taxes that provided $300 million to Microsoft co-founder Paul Allen to build a football/soccer stadium and exhibition center.

That catalyst helped create three Super Bowl teams and an NFL championship for the Seahawks in 2014, as well as an MLS Cup winner for the Sounders in 2016. CenturyLink Field houses fanbases acclaimed as creators of the best home field advantage in their respective sports.

"Magical," said Fred Mendoza, a Seattle lawyer and a key player in the 1997 drama. "How everything worked out is . . . magical."

The series of events that led up to the pivot point is so improbable that Mendoza's invocation of the paranormal is apt. Sounders' birth and growth alone will fill a boxcar with preposterousness.

"There were about 20 things that had to happen the way they did, and were worth about five percent each, in adding up to our success," said Adrian Hanauer, majority owner of the Sounders. "We checked all 20 boxes – 100 percent. It went fantastically well."

The near-perfect outcomes stand in contrast to so-far-futile efforts to return the NBA to Seattle. In the nine years since the Sonics left, no ground has been broken on a new arena, and prospects for the debut of the NHL are still years away with no clear path yet.

"You lose a team, and it's incredibly hard to get it back," said Mendoza, "as we're seeing."

Majority owner, Adrian Hanauer
Photo by Matt Warso

In fact, it was the loss of the Seahawks – for two weeks in 1996 – that triggered the absurd sequence that helped produce two champions.

In 1995, after the first good six weeks of baseball in Mariners history provided not only the franchise's first playoff team, but $380 million of public funds for a new stadium, Seahawks owner Ken Behring wanted similar treatment for a new football stadium.

But his Seahawks were mediocre, and the Legislature told him to drop dead.

So without permission from Seattle or the NFL, he trucked up the franchise's goods from Kirkland and moved to the Los Angeles market left empty by the relocations of the Raiders and Rams. A civil suit and NFL commissioner Paul Tagliabue forced him back to Seattle for the 1996 season.

Allen, owner of the NBA Portland Trail Blazers, was implored by local officials to help out by buying the franchise from Behring, a California real estate developer who bought the team in 1988 from the Nordstrom family.

A hoops guy who didn't know much about football, Allen reluctantly agreed, but with a big stipulation – he would buy the team for $200 million, and throw in another $100 million to help fund a new stadium, but the the public needed to contribute $300 million to help replace a damaged and fading Kingdome.

Since the Legislature was still being pilloried for the Mariners' stadium giveaway in late 1995, a decision was made to put up the stadium funding issue for a statewide public vote. Even in the go-go 1990s replete with federal and state budget surpluses, the idea of voters subsidizing a billionaire's playpen sounded ludicrous.

But lobbyists cobbled together what amounted to a series of user taxes on admission tickets, hotels, motels and car rentals that required no general tax funds. Even so, polls on the subject showed skepticism for public funding, even if no general tax funds were at risk.

Enter Mendoza, a longtime soccer fan who volunteered his professional time to the Washington State Youth Soccer Association. He had been working on a plan with Michael Campbell, head of the Seattle Sports Council, to secure one of the inaugural franchises in Major League Soccer, which would debut in 1996.

Big problem: No natural-grass stadium fit to host pro soccer.

Reading about Allen's football-stadium proposal, he called Bert Kolde, Allen's longtime friend and consigliere. In a subsequent meeting, Mendoza and Campbell asked Kolde what he thought about a plan, in exchange for sharing the stadium, of drawing the electoral support of the state's robust soccer community.

"Gentlemen," Mendoza recalled Kolde saying, "This is a great idea."

Lobbyists rushed to Olympia to re-write the legislation to include pro soccer with pro football. Armed with a commitment from Allen to subsidize the cost of staging the election for $4 million – the first and only such private funding in state history — Mendoza and Campbell whooped when the Senate voted 28-21 to authorize the vote on an open-air stadium on the site to be vacated by the Kingdome.

But the vote was scheduled in less than three months.

Organized by one of Seattle's legendary public relations masters, Bob Gogerty, Mendoza, Kolde and Bob Whitsitt jumped in the Seahawks president's Mercedes and began driving around the state, meeting politicians, community leaders and soccer organizations to seek their support.

Mendoza recalls going to innumerable Saturday morning soccer tournaments, dragging along a box, upon which he would stand with a microphone and a tinny speaker, preaching.

"Heady times," Mendoza said, chuckling. "My law partners asked, 'Are you ever coming back to work?'"

The polls said the eastern side of the state was largely opposed, meaning that the four populous west-side counties – Snohomish, King, Pierce and Thurston, where youth soccer was popular – would have to carry the day.

They did.

A surprisingly high turnout for a single-issue election, 51 percent of eligible voters, approved the measure by a 51.1 percent plurality, a difference of 36,780 votes. The post-election party was scheduled for King Street Station, where Mendoza had arrived early and anxious.

"The Times and P-I endorsed the project, and finally Gov. (Gary) Locke supported it, as did (ex-governor and senator) Dan Evans," he said. "Most businesses liked it, but I was uncertain and real nervous. The early mail returns from the east side showed only 40 percent yes. So we waited late until the King County ballots came in."

That's when wannabe rocker Allen emerged on a stage, guitar in hand, smile on his face. His band, "Grown Men," serenaded the assembled and the party was on.

The overwhelming consensus was that the soccer community was the difference-maker. But it took 12 years before the soccer promise was fulfilled.

The Kingdome had to stay in place until the Mariners exited in mid-1999. Then the Seahawks had to move to Husky Stadium – where Allen originally wanted the team, in a stadium upgraded on his nickel for both teams – for two years before the new stadium opened in 2002.

Mendoza was appointed to the board of directors for the Public Stadium Authority that operates the building, a position he holds today. He was there to assure soccer's interests were heard.

Even though the USL Sounders, owned since 2001 by Hanauer, had the first sports event in the new stadium — "We beat Vancouver 4-1 in front of 25,500 fans; wanna know who scored?" said Hanauer, in the manner of a father witnessing birth – the soccer community grew impatient for the top-tier league.

Shortly after Tod Leiweke was hired by Allen to become Seahawks CEO in 2003, he called Mendoza to have lunch.

"He said, 'Fred, I'm told you're the guy I have to make a speech to,'" Mendoza recalled. "He explained to me that Paul remembers the commitment made to soccer, and the commitment soccer made to him. He said he wanted me to understand that he didn't have permission to pursue MLS until he righted the Seahawks ship.

"He said, 'I'm with you, but I have to do this first. We need some time.'"

By 2006, the Seahawks became NFC champions and made their first Super Bowl. In 2007, MLS Commissioner Don Garber introduced Hanauer, who unsuccessfully pursued a franchise for

Salt Lake City in 2006, to Joe Roth, a big-time Hollywood producer and huge soccer fan.

Roth had choices as to where he would invest, but was aware that the NBA and Seattle were at odds over the Sonics future. When Seattle was awarded an expansion franchise by MLS in November 2007, the Sonics had begun their final season.

Roth said two years ago, "The main reason we chose Seattle was the Sonics were going."

Hanauer, who took over as Sounders majority owner from Ross last year, agreed.

"I decided it was a good time to participate, even at a franchise fee six times what it had been two years earlier," he said, referring to $30 million paid for the Sounders against $5 million for Real Salt Lake. "It was good timing for us, not just because the Sonics were exiting, but the Mariners were struggling, the Seahawks slid back. There wasn't a lot of juice in the market.

"There was definitely a vacuum we were able to fill quickly."

The Sounders, with Allen as a co-investor supplying the Seahawks' business personnel, debuted in March 2009, eight months after the Sonics left. In the first season, they more than doubled the MLS record for attendance in a season. In 2010, Leiweke hired a new Seahawks coach, Pete Carroll, and a new general manager, John Schneider.

By 2013 the Seahawks were again NFC champions, but this time won the Super Bowl. The Sounders signed a world-class American player, Clint Dempsey. By 2014, the Sounders left their five-year partnership with the Seahawks and hired their own soccer-specific front office.

In 2015, Hanauer surrendered his GM role, hired his replacement, Garth Lagerwey, and took over from Roth as majority owner. In midseason 2016, the franchise's only head coach, Sigi Schmid, was fired, replaced by top assistant Brian Schmetzer.

And on a frozen December night in Toronto, the Sounders, who had zero shots on goal, completed a bewildering turnaround with an even more bewildering game to became MLS champions.

Two champions, one stadium, one precarious, preposterous path

"Bart Wiley put it best," Hanauer said of his chief operating officer. "The two best decisions we made as an organization were partnering with Seahawks, and splitting off operations with the Seahawks, to run our own operations and create our own identity.

"The Seahawks had the infrastructure and safety net. All that experience was paramount to launching with success. Tod couldn't have been a better partner, who didn't get enough credit for how successful we were."

It would also appear the state's voters made a good decision in 1997. The bonds used to fund construction will be retired on schedule in 2021.

Hanauer, who fell under soccer's spell in 1976 at the Kingdome's first sports event, the New York Cosmos and Pele vs. the Sounders, still has a hard time believing what has happened.

He recalled leaving the club's Pioneer Square offices in December for the Sounders' victory parade starting at Westlake Center, which drew upward of 50,000 fans.

"I honestly didn't know if anyone was going to show up," he said. "I'm serious. We saw some people walking with Sounders gear, and I was thinking, 'Where are they going? Oh, they're going to the march.'

"Maybe that's my defense mechanism, not wanting to be disappointed. But seeing that throng of people, with the joy, the passion and connection to the Sounders, that really took me aback. It showed me what an important part of this community the Sounders have become."

Not only were there two championships from one stadium ordained by a majority of state voters, the successes also germinated from deep local roots, without anyone noticing.

The three major pro sports ownerships are now led by Seattle natives who went to high school here: Hanauer at Mercer Island, Allen at Lakeside and John Stanton, a Newport High School grad, who took over the Mariners' majority ownership in 2016.

If basketball fan and Seattle native Chris Hansen one day were to acquire ownership of an NBA team he has been seeking since 2011, the Blanchet student and Roosevelt High School grad would make it four.

Given all the business and competitive travails, often emanating from out-of-town ownerships, that attended Seattle's sports franchises in the '70s, '80s and '90s, plus the 2008 loss of the Sonics, June 1997, when the local guys won, was the turn from the valley toward the pinnacles.

pg 42: Morris, up-close and personal
Photo by Lyndsay Radnedge

pg 43: Former majority owner, Joe Roth
Photo by Max Aquino

Chapter Five

The Dark Days
The Second 11 Games

By Ari Liljenwall

Ari Liljenwall is the Sounders beat writer for MLSSoccer.com and a regular co-host on KJR's Radio Cascadia Live Show.

Picking back up with the rough end of the 2016 campaign, the Sounders found themselves with 9 points from their first 13 matches. The haul didn't seem entirely disastrous – after all, that mark was good for top in Cascadia, which included defending champions Portland. It had culminated with a 2-0 win over the San Jose Earthquakes on May 7, a club Sounders had historically not beaten with regular ease. But I'm sure most of the Sounders fanbase remembers the first half of 2016 the same way I do – bad compared to what we'd come to expect.

Everyone will always jump to the story of the miracle Nicolas Lodeiro-fueled turnaround that eventually ended in the MLS Cup victory. But to me, there will always be something funny and weirdly appropriate about the fact that Seattle's first championship came during a season when they played arguably their worst prolonged stretch of soccer as an MLS franchise. Sounders veteran and MLS original Brad Evans said it best talking to reporters at a training session shortly after Seattle had won the Western Conference championship:

"Even in our carpool midway through the year, we always thought this (2016) was going to be a year that [making it to MLS Cup] could

happen. It was always maybe a joke. It was like, 'Yeah, with the ways things have gone, we're probably going to make the Cup.'"

I bring all of this up because the scope of this chapter is to cover the period between Seattle's 2-0 loss at FC Dallas on May 14, 2016 and their 3-0 loss at Sporting Kansas City on July 24 that turned out to be Sigi Schmid's last game as the Sounders coach. And there's really no other way to describe that period aside from saying that it was part of arguably the club's darkest hour in Major League Soccer.

The problem was never all that complicated: The team just couldn't score goals. Even during their lowest points of the season, Sounders were not all that bad defensively. Sure, they leaked some goals at some inopportune times but it could also argued that Stefan Frei was the team's biggest bright spot through this entire stretch.

No, the problem was the attack, which could just never get going. The shutout at FC Dallas on May 14th was followed by another goose egg, this time in a 1-0 loss to the Colorado Rapids at CenturyLink Field. Midfielder Aaron Kovar scored his first MLS goal

in their next match – an away fixture against the New England Revolution – but they still lost that game 2-1. Bad defensive lapses at inopportune moments had doomed them again.

They beat DC United 2-0 at RFK Stadium on June 1, but that was a short-lived high, with their next two MLS matches both 2-0 defeats – first to the New York Red Bulls on June 19, then to New York City FC at CenturyLink on June 25. That game had the added humiliation of being one of the few when Frank Lampard made a contribution to MLS, opening the scoring for his club in the 38th minute. Some controversy ensued about whether the goal was legitimate or not, with even Sigi Schmid weighing in post-game to declare handball. The only real controversy, in hindsight, was the disturbingly aberrant loss in a match played at home in front of at least 50,000 people.

There were occasional signs of life.

A squad of almost entirely Sounders reserve players went to Rio Tinto Stadium on June 28 and succeeded where the first team hadn't in March, beating a first-choice Real Salt Lake squad on penalties to reach the Quarterfinals of the US Open Cup. Goalkeeper Tyler Miller made two stops in the shootout, adding to a stellar performance throughout the night. Only Joao Plata's penalty kick just before halftime beat him across the 120 minutes. Miller had the last laugh as his save on Plata's attempt in the second round of penalties changed the complexion of the shootout. Seattle had equalized early in the second half on a freak mix up at the back which saw Nelson Valdez beat Jeff Attinella to a loose ball outside the the box. Valdez cashed into the empty net for a rare goal and the Sounders wouldn't need any more offense before penalties to secure their advancement. Herculez Gomez, Jordan Morris, and Zach Scott all converted from the spot and Miller added one more stop on Kyle Beckerman for good measure. Erik Friberg ended the shootout after three and a half rounds and by scoring the Sounders' fourth successful spot kick.

Jordan Morris scored one of the highlight reel golazos of the season in a 1-1 draw at Toronto FC four days later. There was also the 5-0 blowout of FC Dallas at CenturyLink on July 13, although most hesitate to count that as much of anything other than the Sounders laying into a largely second-choice lineup fielded by FCD coach Oscar Pareja.

Even so, whatever momentum may have been gained from that victory was swiftly eradicated as the Sounders headed down to Portland for their next match at Providence Park. The second goal from Timbers midfielder Diego Valeri was utterly memorable, scoring the best goal of the day in the 44th minute with a strike from an absolutely ridiculous angle on the right flank to put Portland up 2-0. It was the type of goal that can only go in against you when nothing is going right and that moment can kind of be thought of as the Sounders season to that point in a microcosm.

Chad Marshall would pull one back with a 59th-minute header but the defending on the day was never strong enough to secure a result. Lucas Melano ran at Tyrone Mears on a counter attack in the 64th minute, and the Englishman kept backpedalling until he played Fanendo Adi onside himself. Melano squared for the open striker to tap into the back of the net restoring the two goal advantage. The Sounders never threatened again. At that point they were 6-11-2 and seemed like Western Conference playoff afterthoughts. Anyone who follows MLS knows that the postseason structure is very forgiving and poor early-season results can often be offset by one prolonged hot streak. But I'll admit, at this point in the season, I truly thought the Sounders were going to miss the playoffs for the first time in their MLS history. The hole was just too big.

As far as a tangible low point, you'd have to think that Seattle's next game – a road matchup against Sporting Kansas City on July 24 – will be looked back on as exactly that.

The team had bowed out of the US Open Cup in disappointing fashion four days earlier, losing 4-2 to the LA Galaxy. Schmid had his hands tied with difficult matches at Portland and Kansas City bookending the Quarterfinal, leading to a youthful lineup for the Sounders in their extra trip to Carson. Michael Farfan and Herculez Gomez twice gave Seattle an unexpected lead, but it was a series of uncharacteristic mistakes from Sounders veterans at the back that eventually saw them eliminated from the competition that night. The loss was emotional on its own, with many players feeling the result didn't reflect the effort and grit they'd put into the match. It turned out to be only a setup for the weekend.

Sounders traveled directly from LA to Kansas City following their Open Cup exit. Watching that match at Children's Mercy Park in KC that day, it was obvious that the heat made for absurd, almost comically brutal conditions. Evans would later say that the combination of the humidity and 90-plus degree temperatures made for the toughest elements of any kind that he had ever played in. But both sides had to play in it and to be truthful, only one did.

The Sounders didn't just lose that game, though. They were historically futile, with an 88th-minute garbage-time attempt from Joevin Jones turning out to be the only thing separating them from the dubious distinction of becoming the first team in MLS history to go an entire game without taking a shot. The attack was once again listless. The defending wasn't much better, with right back Tyrone Mears providing the lowlight of the afternoon when he stopped running for a back pass that SKC forward Dom Dwyer stole, subsequently lashing past Frei for the game's last goal and a 3-0 final. At that point, a full-throttle rebuild in the upcoming offseason seemed more likely than any sort of dramatic turnaround and the club announced that they had mutually parted ways with Schmid just days later.

This period will always stand out to me as the toughest stretch the team has endured.

If you had told me following that loss to Sporting Kansas City that this would be the season that would end with Seattle's first championship, I would have called you crazy. Even with Lodeiro coming in, there was simply too much ground to make up. Plus, he certainly came to Seattle with impressive pedigree but were Seattle's problems such that one player could transform them from Western Conference cellar dwellers to championship contenders?

It didn't seem likely. And if it were to happen, it would require a miracle.

WESTERN CONFERENCE STANDINGS							
POSITION	POINTS	TEAM	W	L	T	GF	GA
1	41	FC Dallas	12	6	5	35	31
2	38	Colorado	10	2	8	23	14
3	35	LA Galaxy	9	3	8	34	19
4	31	Sporting KC	9	10	4	27	25
5	31	Real Salt Lake	8	6	7	30	31
6	30	Vancouver	8	8	6	33	35
7	29	Portland	7	7	8	33	33
8	26	San Jose	6	6	8	22	23
9	20	Seattle	6	12	2	20	27
10	19	Houston	4	9	7	23	26

pg 48: Sporting KC scores in Schmid's last game in charge
Photo by Graham Green

pg 49: Herculez Gomez
Photo by Debby Von Winckelmann

Chapter Six

Sigi
The End of an Era

By Steve Clare

Steve Clare is the founder of Prost Amerika and Prost Publishing.

He came in a blaze of PR and glory. He left after reaching the playoffs in each of his first seven seasons.

But after a match in Kansas City where Sounders nearly failed to register a shot, the club issued a press release: Sounders and Sigi Schmid had parted by mutual consent. At that moment, the side had 20 points on the board after 20 games, a point per game unlikely to see them finish anywhere but last place — and certainly see the side fail to reach the playoffs for the first time. To be moderately fair, the side had been playing better than the result indicated – until the Sporting game. There was no shortage of spirit on display by the side in a US Open Cup tie in LA just days before, just a lack of composure in the defensive third.

But by then the vultures were already circling. Some suggested that Schmid would remain while the side were still in the Open Cup, a tournament which has always held more prestige in Seattle than almost everywhere else.

Others had mulled that the writing was on the wall from the minute Garth Lagerwey arrived as General Manager and President of Soccer.

Schmid had built a reasonable working relationship with former General Manager Adrian Hanauer, but it was based on the idea that Schmid knew MLS, and Hanauer knew Seattle and knew Seattle Sounders. It is hard to see any areas of running a football club where there would be any doubt as to which had the expertise. Speculation also suggested the mutual spectre of Joe Roth kept them fairly united.

Lagerwey of course knew MLS and its player base better than anyone.The man who made a small market Real Salt Lake one of the league's giants also came in with a mission to reshape and rebuild the club. Making the squad younger was perhaps his most important mission. Schmid's stock in trade, the part of this industry at which he excels, is plucking players from around the league and making them better players in Seattle than they had ever been elsewhere. His supporters would be suffer from no shortage of evidence with Brad Evans, Chad Marshall and Stefan Frei being exhibits A, B and C. It's not impossible to see where those two methods of filling the squad might clash.

There had been fan pressure on Schmid from some elements of the fanbase annually after every elimination from the playoffs. His

substitutions and his overly defensive tactics particularly in playoff away legs were repeated targets of criticism. His insistence on regularly blaming referees for setbacks also lost some of the older supporters who did not necessarily expect justifications for losing games in a league based on parity.

By the time the side reached 20 points from 20 games in MLS, a tipping point had been reached. Long time tactical critics, critics of the paucity of talent coming through the pipeline and those who simply looked at the league table and had 20/20 vision were all united that the time for change had come.

Ari Liljenwall covers the Sounders for MLSSoccer.com. He stressed that the optics may have played a part in forcing the club's hand:

"I'll always have a lot of respect for Sigi, not just for all of his accomplishments as a coach but also for his professionalism in dealing with the media, which I always appreciated. I think what you saw with his departure from Seattle wasn't necessarily about his ability as a coach, but optics.

"Sometimes change for the sake of change is necessary and with the team struggling the way it was and Sigi being in his eighth season, I think there was a feeling that his message wasn't resonating like it used to and it was time for a change.

"It might not have been entirely fair given that I think Seattle's issues at the time went far beyond just coaching. But given how things turned out with the run the team went on after Brian Schmetzer took over, it's also hard to argue with it in hindsight."

One way of interpreting Liljenwall's words is that Adrian Hanauer and Garth Lagerwey needed to be seen to be doing something. But if Liljenwall did not actually suggest that outright, Matt Pentz, then writing for the Seattle Times, leant more towards the actual need to act, rather than appear to be acting:

Garth Lagerwey and Schmid had a rocky relationship
Photo by Brandon Bleek

"More and more, ownership was convinced that a different voice was required in order to get the best out of the group. Schmid dismisses the idea that he lost the locker room – and I mostly agree with him – but there was just a sense of stagnation, that something big had to change to freshen things up. That, and the gap between Sounders and the playoff spots was widening too far for anybody to ignore."

It was a period when the fanbase's perception of Schmid was being rapidly rewritten. Some accused Schmid of failing to help himself at times, a feeling articulated by Prost Amerika Seattle Editor and lead author on this book, Steven Agen:

"Perhaps the most concerning thing about Sounders' start to 2016 was the lack of answers. Naturally the open Designated Player slot left potential, but few rumors swirled around the club in the spring to kickstart excitement about it. No one could really say for certain why Seattle were underperforming so badly, but Sigi Schmid's points in defense of his team got stranger and stranger as the results got worse.

"Take this gem from his press conference following Sounders' 1-0 loss to LA Galaxy on July 9, after he was asked about if the squad could use reinforcements:

'I think you could always use reinforcements,' Schmid said.

'But if you look at the game today – if you just landed from Mars and you looked at the game and nobody told you what the score was – who do you think the guy from Mars would say who won the game?'

Poor results ended Sigi Schmid's tenure in Seattle, but his inability to provide answers in the press, or even to distract the fanbase from the struggles certainly catalyzed the process."

Within 24 hours though of the announcement of Sigi's departure on July 26, the club announced the arrival of Uruguayan playmaker Nicolas Lodeiro. Lodeiro had been Seattle bound for some time but the clubs had agreed he would stay at his Argentinian side Boca Juniors until they were eliminated from the Copa Libertadores.

Unfortunately for Seattle and Schmid, Boca Juniors kept advancing. They won their Group 3 Qualification section with ease ahead of fellow Argentineans Racing, Bolivar (Bolivia) and Deportivo Cali (Colombia). Paraguay's Cerro Porteño were dispatched 5-2 on aggregate in the last 16. This secured Boca a two-legged tie against top Uruguayan club Nacional to be played on May 12 and 19th.

Boca were 18 minutes from elimination on May 19 until a late Cristian Pavon equaliser sent the game to penalties. 18 minutes only. Lodeiro was a mere one fifth of a soccer game away from being ready to head to the Emerald City in May. But it went to penalties instead.

Boca were trailing 3-2 with two penalties each left. Nacional had scored with all three. Lodeiro was surely on his way to Seattle. Gonzalo Porras missed Nacional's fourth and Santiago Romero missed their fifth. It went to sudden death where Felipe Carballo missed Nacional's third in a row.

Had Nacional not lost their penalty taking boots in such dramatic fashion, Sounders FC would have been able to welcome Lodeiro earlier, seven weeks earlier to be more exact, such was the gap between the quarterfinals and the semifinal.

Those seven weeks proved disastrous for Sounders and fatal for Schmid.

Sounders endured the entire month of June and 24 days of July without Lodeiro. In the period between Boca's comeback penalty kick win and Lodeiro's eventual debut, Sounders lost seven out of ten league games and were eliminated from the Open Cup. They won six out of the next ten after the Uruguayan arrived, accumulating 21 points.

Who is to know what might have happened had Lodeiro arrived earlier? Had Sounders FC recorded the same record in the last ten games, Schmid's last ten, before his arrival as they did the next ten games they would have had 34 points from 20 games, enough to have been top of the opposing Eastern Conference and be within shouting distance of a second successive Supporters Shield. Schmid's side would have been well above the red line that guarantees playoff soccer.

Had Schmid been able to command the talents of Nicolas Lodeiro, who knows whether the same turnaround would have occurred? Schmid was careful to be very respectful of his replacement as coach when I asked him:

"I was looking forward to coaching him and the impact he would bring to the team," he said drily with the implication that he felt it to be so in much stronger words.

Who also, beyond the inner sanctum, knows if the timing of Schmid's dismissal was related to the imminent arrival of the Uruguayan? Did Hanauer and Lagerwey decide it would be negative for the new import to see a coach leave in his first week? All emotions aside, it certainly made sense to introduce the new talent to a locker room on the way up after a bounce rather than on the way down, and about to hit rock bottom.

It also makes sense for the new coach to find the new arrival's best position rather than one who is always 90 minutes away from departure.

In short, if you were going to do it at all, parting ways with Schmid before Lodeiro arrived was the smart thing to do. It also alleviated the new arrival from the heavy burden of saving a man's job. Don Ruiz covered the club for the Tacoma News Tribune and was there when Schmid arrived in 2009. He summed it up perfectly:

"So the coach changed, and so did the results. Dramatically: from death spiral to mountain top. But the causes and effects of life are seldom that clear. And in this case there also was the wildcard of Nicolas Lodeiro, who came about the time Schmid went.

"Certainly, Schmid would have liked to have seen what he might have done with Lodeiro in his 11. But championships always have their element of chemistry, and while we know what Schmetzer plus Lodeiro produced, what Schmid plus Lodeiro might have done will always be a matter of speculation."

However, notwithstanding the machinations that led to his dismissal, it is only fair to look back on Schmid's achievements.

Schmid redefined the standard expected of expansion teams. Making the playoffs in his first year was an amazing achievement. As if that wasn't enough, he scooped the US Open Cup on hostile enemy territory.

He proved MLS playoff soccer was no fluke by repeating the feat in 2010, and in 2011 by which time Cascadia neighbours Portland and Vancouver were making the Western Conference notably more competitive. More Open Cup wins were to follow as Sounders practically wrote their name on the trophy.

Becoming a victim of his own success, people began to expect more than merely making the playoffs. Their failure to advance deep into the postseason attracted criticism until one memorable night at the Rio Tinto Stadium in Utah, Honduran Mario Martínez

wrote himself into Sounders folklore by scoring an 81st minute winner against RSL in a hitherto scoreless tie in 2012.

They made the Conference Championships in 2014 when they beat FC Dallas and lost to LA Galaxy only on the away goals rule. In the years around that progress, they stuttered at the round before. The 2013 loss to Portland Timbers was especially painful as the Oregon side were only in their third year in MLS, they were Seattle's fiercest local rivals, they won both legs and the home tie was played on the backdrop of NFL Lines on the Seattle pitch. You could not have scripted a worse scenario for Sounders FC; second class citizens in their stadium, and beaten by little brother in front of a national television audience.

If Sounders had fired Sigi Schmid at that point, few could have complained. I wasn't one of those clamouring for it, but I was in the minority and in no way thought those on the other side of that argument were being unreasonable.

His 100% record of making the playoffs continued amidst a feeling that it was no longer enough. The 2015 loss was to Dallas on penalties. However, few would claim that it marked progress as Dallas had really outplayed them over the 180 minutes and Sounders had moved a round further the year before. Moreover, in the more successful 2014 year, Sounders had also won the US Open Cup. It created a sense that reversed the notion that Sounders were going forward every year under Schmid. They were going backwards. Worst of all, the notion that expansion clubs take time to adapt had been blown out the water by Portland winning the MLS Cup in 2015.

Further insult was added by the manner of their Open Cup elimination. Portland Timbers had come to Tukwila and beaten the side, the Open Cup holders, in their own backyard, in their own favoured competition. The club were further disgraced by the antics of Clint Dempsey who grabbed and ripped up the referee's red card.

Sounders' league form dipped significantly after that night. Of course no-one but Dempsey can take responsibility for his own behaviour, but the slump in form thereafter added fuel to the viewpoint that Schmid was not as in control of his players as he once had been. Those who were already predisposed to hostility to Schmid found a way to use the incident against him. That set the scene for the 2016 season which was to be Schmid's last.

Behind the scenes there had been personnel changes that heaped further pressure on him. Adrian Hanauer had replaced Joe Roth as Majority Owner. Garth Lagerwey stepped into Hanauer's shoes. There was a reasonable argument that both Roth and Hanauer had looked into their own performances rather than hide behind the coach. They deserve praise for that because not many others in the notoriously disloyal sport would have acted so nobly. While that kept Schmid in charge another year, there was no hiding place thereafter. The Front Office had displayed immense loyalty to him, and suggested by their actions that a more supportive and operational structure behind Schmid would maximise his chances of success. And if they didn't, there would be nobody else to blame.

The man had arrived in a blaze of publicity in the days when, if MLS had a record, the new franchise would break it. There can be no bigger statement than going out and poaching the man who coached the current MLS Champions. I met the then Columbus Crew GM Brian Bliss at a Red Bulls game in 2008, and (after finding out I came from Seattle) told me "....if you want him, you're going to get him. There's nothing we can do to stop you." Bliss was rueful but he knew an earthquake was coming to Major League Soccer.

There was always something about Schmid that didn't quite fit in with in with this brash PR machine Sounders cultivated. Schmid brought an abundance of personality to the Emerald City. At his opening press conference, Schmid burst into tears when thinking about family matters which certainly did not into the agenda set out for the day.

What Seattle got was a man who knew Major League Soccer as well as anyone, along with his great rival Bruce Arena. There is a myth about Schmid that it is probably time to explode and that is the myth that all he achieved was somehow inevitable.

Many assumed that playoff soccer was automatic because Sounders had large attendances. The club PR in those days was fixated on the attendance figure and made the connection that the ability to attract great crowds equated to being a large club which equated to success on the field.

It may be true in Spain where Barcelona and Real Madrid have used a combination of success and politics to attract support and therefore money. It may be true in a league like Italy where large resources allow you to outspend less well supported rivals by buying their best players to weaken the opposition. It's certainly true in England where wealthy individuals from Russia and the Gulf States can buy instant EPL titles, (and arguably even World Cups). It is palpably not true in Major League Soccer where the salary cap prevents any club buying decades of dominance. Decades of dominance have to be earned. And Schmid's Sounders earned its decade.

In 2009, it was a remarkable achievement to make the playoff with a reluctant Swede who often ploughed his own field during games, several MLS journeymen unwanted elsewhere, six holdovers from USL and one-off characters from different ends of the age spectrum like Steve Zakuani and Kasey Keller. Bringing that disparate collection into a coherent unit so quickly was probably Schmid's crowing and least likely achievement. Winning the Open Cup on the road as an underdog against one of the league's marquee names was the icing on that cake and, for those of us in RFK Stadium that night, it felt as much like an underdog triumph as anything done since.

Pressure only intensifies when you are a success. Schmid brought more silverware with Open Cups in front of home crowds, again breaking attendance records. As that was getting old, he added a Cascadia Cup in his first attempt at it. There was Champions League soccer to boot. But as appreciation rose for the man, expectations rose for the club.

More coconuts were knocked off their perches. He took his first Champions League point, the first MLS playoff victory, increasing recognition for Sounders players at international level – and then finally the Holy Grail for many Seattle fans, the first Supporters' Shield.

None of that was inevitable for a club joining in the 21st Century. Only half of it has happened in Toronto to this day. Other clubs like Portland and Montreal have hit highs and then receded from them very quickly. Schmid achieved it all and kept doing it. He perhaps was given less credit than he deserved because the expectations were raised too high.

Nonetheless, it is reasonable to ask if any other coach would have achieved in those opening years what he did with Sounders FC.

The answer I believe is no. For that, he should always return to the Emerald City a hero.

pg 57: Best of Schmates

pg 58: Schmid accepting MLS award from Adrian Hanauer

pg 59: Schmid pondering changes
Photos by Max Aquino

Chapter Seven

Schmetzer and Lodeiro Steady the Ship

By Andrew Harvey

Andrew Harvey writes for Sportspress Northwest (sportspressnw.com) and is a regular co-host on KJR's Radio Cascadia Live.

Interim head coach Brian Schmetzer's first game in charge was a tall order, squaring off against an LA Galaxy team that had just embarrassed the club in the Open Cup and had shut out Seattle in a 1-0 win at CenturyLink Field three weeks prior.

In Schmetzer's first post-practice media scrum as the interim head coach, he promised change.

"I can't guarantee that it's going to happen fast, but we're preparing for it now," Schmetzer said. "We're going to make sure that we get a plan in place for the next couple of weeks to maximize our chance of winning and incorporating guys with the group.

"We're going to make sure that we hold people accountable."

The acquisition of Uruguayan midfielder Nicolas Lodeiro from Boca Juniors provided a big boost. Sounders GM Garth Lagerwey hailed the signing as the emblem of a new philosophical and tactical shift for the club:

"Philosophically, this is a new beginning for us," Lagerwey said. "This is an opportunity for us to play with the ball on the ground, to be a possession-based team, to be a passing team, to be a creative attacking team. To say that the solution is not to sign another attacker, but to sign a midfielder who can change the game.

"I think it's an exciting way to play, a way that our fans want to see. I also think that it is the way of the modern MLS. The league is increasingly technical, continues to add higher numbers of good players . . . It's going to be a higher level of soccer, and we needed a higher level of player in the middle of our team to put us on level footing with the other teams."

Lodeiro's contributions began before he even took the pitch for Seattle. Four days after his arrival, Lodeiro was waiting in the team dressing room in the bowels of CenturyLink Field as his new club prepared to face the third-place Galaxy. While the team was getting dressed, someone had tuned a stereo to the team's usual pregame playlist.

Lodeiro left his locker and turned off the music, announcing to his new teammates that the situation was dire and that greater focus was required.

Brian Schmetzer chats to then Quakes coach Dom Kinnear
Photo by Lyndsay Radnedge

The message got through. Seattle drew LA 1-1 thanks to Cristian Roldan's second professional goal, while Lodeiro looked like the smartest man on the pitch, swarming all over the field and at times sending passes to areas that his teammates did not yet understand would be open.

The result against the Galaxy bolstered the team's confidence. Then-captain Brad Evans noted the difference in the team's attitude since Schmetzer took over and Lodeiro arrived.

"Coming in after (the Sporting Kansas City loss) was massively disappointing, and nobody knew what was coming the next week," Evans said August 4. "The morale, I thought, had always remained the same. Guys came out the next day and worked extremely hard, but I think the morale has been different now that there has been a change.

"Maybe I was just blind, or was used to guys coming in every week and whatever happened on the weekend happened. But now things are different. There's a sense of urgency now. Maybe I was missing something that was there, but we're in a good spot now."

The following week, his new club had caught up with Lodeiro's capabilities. The newcomer notched two assists in a 3-1 drubbing of Orlando City on the road that saw Clint Dempsey score a hat trick as rookie forward Jordan Morris finally came into his own and gained greater confidence in distributing the ball inside the penalty area.

Wins followed at home against Real Salt Lake and the Portland Timbers, the former of which saw Lodeiro score his first league goal, while the Cascadian rivals fell victim to another Lodeiro assist.

The Uruguayan also won a crucial point for the Sounders on the road August 24, scoring in the fourth minute of stoppage time as Seattle clawed out a 1-1 draw against the Houston Dynamo, stretching Seattle's unbeaten run to five matches since Schmetzer took charge.

Then, on August 26, two days before a road clash with the Portland Timbers, the club revealed shocking news: Clint Dempsey had been diagnosed with an irregular heartbeat, and would be unavailable for an indeterminate amount of time.

The blow removed one of Seattle's most potent weapons. Dempsey had scored five goals since Schmid was fired, and seemed to be gelling well after returning from USMNT duty for the Copa America.

Now, he would be absent for a pair of crucial matches against the Timbers and a subsequent road match against the San Jose Earthquakes, both sitting one point above Seattle and the red line.

Portland jumped on the Sounders August 28, punching in four first half goals and dismantling the Sounders' hopes. At half-time, Schmetzer's message was simple, according to Evans:

"Schmetzer came in and said, 'We're going to do one thing,'" Evans recounted. "We're going to play for the badge. If you don't do that, I'll take you off.'"

The loss had one bright side: the return of Roman Torres, who appeared as a substitute for the first time since tearing his ACL in September.

After the game, the club seemed disappointed but determined. The determination resulted in another positive result in San Jose, when Lodeiro stole another point for Seattle by scoring on an 80th minute free kick that was Seattle's only shot on goal.

The Lodeiro effect was in full swing. The midfielder recorded a goal or an assist in eight of his first nine matches as a Sounder, earning an overwhelming percent of the vote to be named the MLS Player of the Month in August.

As the calendar rolled into September, Morris' maturation continued paying dividends. The youngster dove onto a cross from Lodeiro for a late game-winner against the Vancouver Whitecaps September 17, then scored two goals in a sensational 4-2 comeback win on the road against the LA Galaxy September 25.

Seattle had not beaten LA on the road since 2009. The signature victory put the club within three points of the red line, a far cry from the club that looked dead on arrival 20 matches into the season.

A Chad Marshall header lifted Seattle over the Chicago Fire and into playoff position September 28. For the first time in 2016, Seattle would control its own playoff destiny. The new circumstances lifted spirits, even while the news filtered down that Dempsey was ruled out for the season due to his heart condition.

As the final matches of the season ticked away, Seattle did enough to stay above the red line despite stumbling in a 0-0 draw at home against Houston and losing on a late goal at FC Dallas.

When decision day rolled around on October 23, Seattle had the opportunity to clinch a playoff spot with a win against Real Salt Lake. A loss or tie, though, would put the playoffs and the comeback season in jeopardy.

The RSL match was a sloppy affair, with both sides conceding goals within the first five minutes and struggling to maintain possession. Seattle climbed on top in the 31st minute when Roldan scored his fourth goal of the season, cleaning up a rebound from a corner kick.

The Sounders managed to defend the lead through the final whistle, capping off an 8-2-4 run that seen them rise from ninth place in the Western Conference to fourth and earn home field advantage in the knockout round against Sporting Kansas City.

Seattle had gone from the most downtrodden team in the league to a club that few teams wanted to face, and they were hitting their stride at the perfect moment.

Chapter Eight

In the Nic of Time
Lodeiro Arrives

By Steven Agen

Steven Agen is the Seattle Editor for Prost Amerika and founder of Radio Cascadia.

From Nicolas Lodeiro's first moments with the Seattle Sounders, it was clear that he was something special.

Making his debut in Brian Schmetzer's first match in charge of the club, Sounders' performance on the day personified Lodeiro's contribution to the team. Despite only drawing 1-1 with LA Galaxy, Seattle put on an attacking barrage that lasted from minute one to ninety.

Robbie Keane's chip nearly stole all three points for the visitors in stoppage time; such a result would have aligned with the rest of the season up until that point. However, it was abundantly clear that something, something was different. Lodeiro was different. He didn't look like some of the other stars in the league, drifting in and out of the match. He was always present, ready to pounce. If it wasn't for several huge missed chances from Jordan Morris, Sounders would have a had a win over a Western Conference playoff team for only the second time all season.

After picking up four points from a possible twelve to start the 2016 campaign, Sigi Schmid had switched things up in Sounders' 1-1 draw at Houston on April 10th. The match saw Seattle field a 4-3-3 formation that would become the new normal until the end of Schmid's tenure. He opted for the set up 13 times out of his final 16 matches with club.

Whether Nicolas Lodeiro would have fit into Schmid's 4-3-3 is a matter of open debate. So too is whether Schmid would have arrived upon the 4-2-3-1 formation Brian Schmetzer opted for as soon as he took charge of the club.

What can be said for certain is that Schmid's 4-3-3 didn't work. Seattle posted a 3-9-2 record when starting in the formation and the stats only got worse from there. Sounders failed to score in six of those thirteen games, and kept clean sheets in only two. If we consider the anomalous 5-0 win over short-handed FC Dallas as an outlier, Sounders scored only nine goals while allowing 19 in the other 12 matches in the 4-3-3 formation.

What can also be said is that Schmetzer and Lodeiro's new set up did work, and it worked right away. Clint Dempsey played centrally with Morris up top and Lodeiro in a free role on the right, and all of sudden the Seattle attack went from anemic to lethal. The first half of the season hadn't provided Seattle with more than three

Nicolas Lodeiro's arrival turned the season around
Photo by Matt Warso

positive results in a row. After Lodeiro's arrival, Seattle rattled off five straight unbeaten matches and lost only one of Lodeiro's first eleven games with the club. Lodeiro and Dempsey opened up space for each other.

The new arrival picked up his first two assists for the club in the trip to Orlando following the draw with LA as Dempsey recorded a hat trick. Twice Dempsey tapped into an empty net, such was the level of control Sounders' offense exerted in Florida.

The newest Designated Player in Cascadia was lighting it up, but not in the way stars of MLS normally tend to. Some of the very best players on the world, take Lionel Messi for example, will drift in and out of a match. They play on the ebbs and flows of the ninety minutes, and pick and choose moments to exert themselves.

Playmakers in MLS tend to follow this mold. Giovinco does it. So did Steven Gerrard in his short stretch in the US. Federico Higuain is another example.

Not Nicolas Lodeiro, though. Lodeiro, from his first match in Seattle, showed a relentless determination throughout its entirety. And so far, that's been the defining characteristic of Lodeiro's time in MLS.

It's not just his silky-smooth through balls, or his ability to pop up anywhere necessary in the attacking half that instantly endeared him to the Sounder faithful. It's not just his off-the-charts set piece taking or the way he turned the club's form around.

It's about the way Nicolas Lodeiro approaches the game of soccer. Every ball is worth chasing down, every opponent closed down, every potential for opportunity seized upon. To watch Lodeiro play soccer is to watch a man on a mission.

Now just to be clear, there is no suggestion that Lodeiro is in the same league as Messi. Messi has Neymar and a few other decent players around him. They rarely look at league tables and see 20 points from 20 games. Being realistic, Lodeiro's initial effort was an indication of how far the team had slipped, so far that the playmaker felt he had to cover the ground, close down the keeper and polish the boots as well. It is indicative of the man but as much of the environment he stepped into.

It is not a level of activity sustainable for more than a few games and is designed to set an example, to get more out of other players by leading the way; perhaps the most major shortcoming in Ljungberg's tenure in Seattle. In that he succeeded.

Perhaps MLS is still just a young league, and our fans are flattered by efforts that Europeans would deem unnecessary. However, a more believable narrative exists. The league has a history of bringing in prima donnas and aging world superstars who don't tend to exert themselves in the way that, say, a Jordan Morris does during an average soccer game.

Seeing the team's new star stoop to the level of closing down the goalkeeper, of chasing down a hopeless long ball was new for Sounders fans who'd grown accustomed to the likes of Freddie Ljungberg, Fredy Montero, Blaise Nkufo and even Clint Dempsey.

Lodeiro's arrival galvanized Sounders, but it wasn't his raw soccer ability that turned their season around. It was his attitude and his effort. He put Sounders on his back and carried them to the promised land, and he did it by setting an example of how unglamorous dirty work, selflessness and relentless determination could take the team to the next level. All of the tricks, skills, and goals will always be brilliant, but they might not ever match what the mentality Lodeiro provided to Sounders in the summer of 2016.

pg 69: Lodeiro singing in the rain
Photo by Max Aquino

pg 70: Capo on his stand
Photo by Max Aquino

pg 71: Tyrone Mears applauds the crowd
Photo by Brandon Bleek

Chapter Nine

SKC Playoff Fortune Favors the Rave (Green)

By Steven Agen

Steven Agen is the Seattle Editor for Prost Amerika and founder of Radio Cascadia.

Sporting Kansas City

And so, with their victory over Real Salt Lake on Decision Day, Brian Schmetzer's Sounders had beaten all odds to make the playoffs. After taking 20 points from their first 20 matches, Seattle finished the season on a tear of (W-D-L) 8-4-2. Only a loss at rival Portland and to Supporter's Shield winners FC Dallas on the penultimate weekend of the season blemished Schmetzer's record.

With the playoff berth secured, the fanbase breathed a collective sigh of relief. The streak of consecutive postseason appearances since joining MLS would live on, and its survival ensured that even a quick playoff exit would be soon forgotten by friends and enemies alike. The cherry on top was landing in the fourth seed in the Western Conference bracket. Sounders hadn't just limped into the MLS Cup playoffs – they'd earned themselves a home match.

The one man who couldn't breathe easily yet was Brian Schmetzer. Despite posting the second-best record in MLS from Matchday 20 on, he had not yet seen the removal of the word "interim" next to his title of head coach. Garth Lagerwey's silence spoke volumes: While the consensus among the fanbase was that Sounders had

done enough in 2016 just by recovering from their horrendous start, Schmetzer knew that only postseason success would guarantee his position on the sidelines beyond that.

Sounders' first opportunity to definitively prove Schmetzer's worth would come against none other than fifth-seeded Sporting Kansas City. The sides had not met since their July 24th encounter which culminated in the sacking of Sigi Schmid. Sounders fans know that game by a simpler moniker: rock bottom. The chance to show how far they'd come from the sweltering heat and oppressive dysfunction of that day in Kansas City added meaning to a match that otherwise ostensibly existed to provide semifinal round fodder for conference leaders Dallas and Colorado.

Knockout Round: Seattle Sounders 1 : 0 Sporting KC

36,151 fans piled into CenturyLink Field on that rainy Thursday night in late October and witnessed one of the most controversial matches in MLS Cup playoff history. Brian Schmetzer went a long ways towards earning his job, Nelson Valdez broke his scoring drought and Benny Feilhaber gave a memorably sarcastic interview after the match, but in retelling this night full of storylines, the only

SKC claimed every big call went against them in the playoff
Photo by Max Aquino

reasonable place to begin is with Sporting KC head coach Peter Vermes.

Soon after the full-time whistle, Vermes walked into his press conference and delivered this opening statement:

"I hope that you don't omit anything that I say here. I mean that. So I'm going to start out first by saying this: I want to congratulate Seattle for moving on. Unfortunately the game was one in which we scored and our guy was onsides, they scored and their guy was offside. Unfortunately [Osvaldo] Alonso for them should've been thrown out of the game, which would've changed the game. There were three plays within the game that would've completely changed the match.

"Where I would start is two and a half weeks ago, we played in Salt Lake and that same center referee did that game as well. In the 86th minute we had a penalty kick – 100 percent a penalty kick. Not just my assessment, but the assessment of PRO, Peter Walton, as well – 100 percent a penalty kick and he doesn't call it. If we score that goal and go on to win that game, we get three points, we're not sitting here today, we're sitting in Kansas City playing this game. So it's coincidental to me that the referee tonight makes another...I can't even understand how you don't give Alonso the second yellow card, which puts him out of the game. They're then playing a man down and now we're in a position to obviously control the game even more so than we did.

"I'm a guy that tries to do my best when evaluating a match. The statistics don't lie in this game. We dominated the game from beginning to end. Like I said, they scored their goal on an offside play, referee misses it and it changes the outcome of the game. I will tell you, in my opinion, and for our organization, I think that PRO and Major League Soccer owe our club an absolute apology because this game was taken away from us today. Our players gave everything they had. We came into a class organization, great fan base, unbelievable environment...we controlled the game. It is what it is. We didn't come in and bunker in and try to sit back and try to muck up the game. We came to play and demonstrated that on the field, but unfortunately because of decisions that were made by the referees...it's amazing, all four of them. The center and the fourth make the decision in not giving the second yellow, at a minimum, to Alonso, which would've put him out of the game. Then the two [assistant referees], one on each side – one called us offside and the other called them onsides.

"I don't know what else to say except that I'm extremely proud of my team and the way that they played. They gave everything. The unfortunate thing is we walk away with an incredibly bad taste in our mouth from the perspective of we didn't lose the game – we got the game taken away from us. And I'll say it again: I believe PRO and the league owe our club an apology."

Vermes addressed four controversial moments across two matches in his monologue. Going through them sequentially, we begin with the no-penalty kick decision from referee Ishmael Elfath in Sporting KC's 0-0 draw at Real Salt Lake on October 16th. While the play in question actually happened in the 78th minute rather than the 87th, it does appear that RSL midfielder Jordan Allen hacked across Benny Feilhaber's legs in the penalty area without touching the ball. Elfath may have believed that Feilhaber dragged his left leg on purpose in order fall down and win the penalty, but regardless the contact from Allen was sufficiently egregious for him to point to the spot.

It's impossible to say if all of the results in the league from October 16th on would have stayed the same if Sporting KC took three points in Utah instead of one. It is undeniably true that, if they had, Sporting would have beaten Sounders to the fourth seed in the West with 49 points to Seattle's 48. Vermes' first point in defense of his squad was the most surprising and most difficult to prove, but it is simple enough to see the merit in the case he made.

The other three points of contention were more clear than the first. Matt Besler was offside as he put Sporting KC ahead in the 53rd minute, but he was less offside than Nelson Valdez was when he scored in the 88th minute. Alonso's challenge on Feilhaber on 68 minutes deserved a card in virtually any context, and particularly when stopping a promising counter attack. Even just a yellow would have seen Sounders' captain dismissed for the last 23 (and maybe 53) minutes of the match.

Peter Vermes had a case, and an awfully good one at that. It is difficult to find another playoff match in recent memory with as much controversy attached to it as this one. Four separate calls over an eleven day span certainly impacted Sporting KC's ability to advance from the Knockout Round. The fact that center referee Ishmael Elfath was ultimately responsible for each decision only added to the drama.

The fifth controversial point Vermes touched on wasn't an officiating decision, but an opinion. In repeatedly declaring that Sporting KC outplayed Seattle on that night, he made his simplest statement and the easiest of the bunch to prove.

The first minutes of the match were dominated by Paolo Nagamura and his two ferocious strikes on goal and the important saves from Stefan Frei to keep them out, punctuated by Graham Zusi's follow-up shot that ricocheted out off the base of the post on 10'. Sporting's dominance continued and Frei's touch on an Ellis redirection was the only thing keeping the visitors out on 32'. Ten minutes later Feilhaber again nearly put Sporting in front.

It was seven minutes after the restart when Besler put the ball in the net, only to see linesman Corey Parker's flag in the air declaring offside. The decision was, as mentioned, extremely tight. However given Valdez's goal later on Sounders could have had few complaints if it had been given, and the lead would certainly

have been no more than Sporting deserved for almost an hour of dominance.

Even after Feilhaber suffered Alonso's red card-worthy challenge, Sporting's playmaker fashioned another great opportunity. The outstretched left leg of Stefan Frei was the only thing in Feilhaber's way after he danced by several Sounders in the area on 79'. It was only after this tremendous attacking display that Sporting eventually conceded to Valdez's offside header and crashed out of the playoffs.

This isn't to say Seattle didn't have a part in securing their advancement, or that they didn't deserve it.

Joevin Jones still had to put in a perfect cross for the offside Valdez to finish. Valdez still had to break a year-long MLS goal scoring drought to put Sounders through. And most importantly, Stefan Frei had the finest performance of his career up to that point in keeping Sporting off the board. The Swiss-born goalkeeper made seven saves en route to being named Man of the Match.

All the storylines outside of the Seattle camp seemed to be about SKC, the drama, and the injustice of the officiating.

On the inside, it was completely different. While Sounders were preparing for Dallas, their fans were celebrating – it might not have been pretty, but the turnaround from July 24th had been officially and emphatically completed. Whether or not Sounders deserved to go through wasn't really important. Almost every team needs some moment of fortune or serendipity on their way to an MLS Cup victory, and Seattle had theirs against Sporting KC.

Chapter Ten

Eight Minutes
That Changed Sounders Forever

By Steven Agen

Steven Agen is the Seattle Editor for Prost Amerika and founder of Radio Cascadia.

FC Dallas

While it may have seemed to some as if the storylines following the Knockout Round disproportionately revolved around Sporting Kansas City, there were no questions about the legitimacy of FC Dallas' domination of media attention in the short build up to the Western Conference Semifinals. When Dallas claimed the 2016 US Open Cup with a 4-2 win over New England Revolution, they ended a 19 year trophy drought dating to the 1997 Open Cup. After their cup triumph on September 13th, they proceeded to finish the last five matches of the regular season unbeaten and won the Supporters' Shield for the first time in club history. Their stretch included a come-from-behind 2-1 win over Seattle in Frisco. Particularly given that their previous meeting was a 5-0 Sounders drubbing over a Dallas B-team in July, most interpreted it as decent indication of the relative strength of the sides. It was the only match between them involving Lodeiro, after all.

Brian Schmetzer had his first MLS playoff victory as Sounders interim head coach, but would have to face another playoff match with that tag attached. With the first leg of the Dallas series taking place only three days after the Knockout Round, there was hardly

time to formally introduce him as head coach in that narrow window even if the Front Office desired to.

His charges had made it through the Knockout Round, but given the manner in which they advanced against Sporting KC it was difficult to properly judge playoff expectations for them going forward. Sounders had defended well and Frei had the game of his life, but it would take more than that to oust Dallas over two legs. There was a feeling that Schmetzer's Sounders hadn't quite gotten to show their playoff posture or potential yet, such was the grind against Sporting.

Certainly Dallas were the favorites – it would be hard for anyone chasing a treble not to be – but the series history made it more compelling than that.

Seattle had eliminated Dallas on away goals following their Shield-winning campaign in 2014 before the Hoops returned the favor after penalties in 2015. Getting to see two of the most successful clubs in the conference go at it in the playoffs in three consecutive years was a rare treat for MLS. With Dallas having won the most recent series between them and now coming in on the heels of

Sounders scored three goals in eight memorable minutes
Photo by Max Aquino

winning two trophies, the rubber match seemed to be there for them to perhaps finally show they'd well and truly overcome Seattle after the disappointment in 2014. The first leg of the 2016 Western Conference Semifinals was the perfect opportunity, as well; Sounders were playing their third important match in a week, even if they were at home. FC Dallas on a week's rest were formidable front-runners.

Western Conference Semifinals: 1st Leg — Sounders FC 3 : 0 FC Dallas

Brian Schmetzer kept his lineup unchanged from Sunday's match against Real Salt Lake to Thursday's against Sporting KC, and his selection for the first leg of the Dallas series would only feature two rotations. Zach Scott replaced Roman Torres; a third match in seven days deemed an unnecessary risk for the centerback freshly recovered from an ACL tear.

After scoring on Decision Day and then starting against Sporting KC, Alvaro Fernandez made his way to the bench with the suddenly in-form Nelson Valdez taking his place. Jordan Morris moved back into a left wing position to allow Valdez to play up top. Fernandez, at age 31, wasn't ever going to be fit for three starts in a short span. Despite his Designated Player tag Valdez would likely not have been considered for a place in Sunday's starting eleven before scoring the winner on Thursday. That swap looked both efficient and elegant on paper when the starting lineups were announced before the match, and nearly paid off right away.

Seattle nearly scored early on another cold, rainy night at CenturyLink Field. 37,073 were in attendance this time as Nelson Valdez nearly turned home a Morris cross on four minutes. Dallas goalkeeper Chris Seitz kept the ball out from close range as pundits wondered if the sequence would shock the sleepy visitors awake. Erik Friberg then collected a clearance from a Sounders corner at the top of the box and fired low towards the left-hand post on 27 minutes, and it took two attempts from Matt Hedges to fully clear the ball away. He may have kept the score level but it was clear that Dallas still weren't firing on all cylinders.

Some of Dallas' early struggles may have been due to the atmosphere in Seattle, but more pronounced was the effect of the unfamiliar formation Dallas head coach Oscar Pareja opted for. His side reached half time at 0-0 but hardly ever looked comfortable in the odd set up, which Opta described as a 5-3-2.

So Seattle had outplayed Dallas for a half but they hadn't even amassed a lead with their superiority, and conventional wisdom held that Dallas couldn't possibly be so off the pace in the second period. The match, the night, the series, the rubber match – it was still all about treble-chasing FC Dallas and whether or not Sounders could get something to cling to on the way back to Frisco.

Eight minutes that changed Sounders forever

Sounders began the second half much as they did the first — on the front foot and goal-dangerous. This time there was a reward for their early chance, as Joevin Jones crossed from space on the left and connected with Nelson Valdez for the second time in four days. Chris Seitz threw himself at ball but couldn't get a hand to it, and Maynor Figueroa couldn't outjump Valdez on the far post. The Paraguayan headed past Seitz and celebrated with the Brougham End. On 50 minutes, Sounders led double-winners FC Dallas 1-0.

CenturyLink Field lit up when Valdez nodded home, and a difficult atmosphere became exponentially more hostile. Whether the crowd was the architect of Dallas' demise or it was their own inability to regroup and right themselves after conceding the opener, the visitors fell apart as Sounders grew ever more rampant.

Two minutes after the opener, Jones was free on the left wing again and crossed for an even-more-unmarked Jordan Morris.

Morris headed that opportunity over, but the same leak had sprung twice in quick succession for Dallas. Most concerning was their visible lack of body language or emotional response after the chance on 52 minutes. No one on the back line looked prepared to take initiative and show the leadership necessary to calm the team. It was still only 1-0 but at that moment it became clear that Dallas were rattled and that their composure wasn't about to immediately resurface.

Five minutes after the opener, a pass for Nelson Valdez at midfield slipped by everyone and Morris was the first to it on the left flank. Nobody stepped up to challenge Morris with any authority as he sliced into the area, and again it was Maynor Figueroa out of position on the far right post. This time he watched Morris and the ball instead of marking Nicolas Lodeiro behind him, and Morris' low cross left the Uruguayan to tap into an empty net for a 2-0 lead after two goals in five minutes from the Seattle left hand side. Hands went to heads and eyes to feet again for the Dallas defenders. Again no one would claim responsibility for the back line and try to snap them back into reality. Dallas were shell shocked.

For a moment it looked like Dallas might have a had response soon after the kickoff. Former Timber Maxi Urruti earned a corner and the visitors streamed forward to try and grab one back off of a set piece. However when Frei corralled the ball and looked to counter, those same Dallas defenders failed to sense the approaching danger.

Frei distributed to Joevin Jones on the left side. As Jones picked out Lodeiro running unmarked past midfield and played a through ball for him, the men in red were still jogging into position with their backs to the play, caught completely unawares. Lodeiro latched onto the ball and slammed it past Seitz for his brace and a 3-0 Seattle lead on the night. The stadium had twice erupted on the night, but 3-0 brought with it sheer pandemonium. Sounders fans cheered not just for the goal, but also for the end of shattered tired

old narratives and for their newly-found poll position in the race for MLS Cup. They weren't just going through to the Conference Finals, they were doing it by smashing the best team in the league in a manner never before seen in Seattle.

Before the 2016 Western Conference Semifinals, Sounders had played 15 aggregate series since joining MLS. Nine of these were MLS Cup playoff series, and six were at various stages of the CONCACAF Champions League. All of these series have one thing in common, one fatal flaw that has dogged Seattle more so than any other – Sounders never led by multiple goals in any of them. Not after the end of a leg, or after the end of the aggregate series. No, Sounders simply never, at any point, ever led an aggregate series by more than a single goal in their first 15 tries at it.

Brian Schmetzer played down the idea that gunning for a multi-goal lead was always in the cards for Seattle, but admitted postgame that he "talked with one of my owners earlier about, after we scored the first [goal], could we go out and score another."

Sounders General Manager and President of Soccer Garth Lagerwey had commented numerous times to the media in the weeks leading up to the Dallas series that the Front Office was more interested in seeing the style in which Schmetzer's team played rather than the results they earned towards the end of the season and into the playoffs. Given the "interim" tag in his title one was left to wonder how important Schmetzer's approach was following Valdez's goal, both in securing his job and in helping Sounders along in their playoff series.

This wasn't just a surprise or an upset or a shock, it flipped the script on seven years of aggregate soccer humiliation. All of the mockery about Sounders' inability to find playoff success, about their failure to perform best in the biggest moments, about their lack of ruthlessness and inability to figure out playoff soccer, about their sheer naivety and blatant lack of results, seemed to lift off of the collective shoulders of the fanbase in one big heave. These weren't the 'bottom of the West Sounders' from July anymore. Nor were these the upstart Sounders that earned a playoff berth on Decision Day, or the gritty Sounders deemed lucky to advance past Sporting KC. These were playoff-capable Sounders, previously unseen and now fresh off eliminating treble-chasing Dallas. And finally, with their arrival, there was no doubt as to who the story was about in the 2016 MLS Cup playoffs.

Seitz came up big to keep Morris out from the top of the box on the hour mark, or Dallas would have returned to Texas trailing 4-0. Instead, the stop finally breathed life into the Hoops and they raised their level to play for the remainder of the game. Former Sounders captain Mauro Rosales subbed on and threatened from set pieces several times, but Dallas' improvement merely ensured that they would see the match out at 3-0.

pg 84: Lodeiro enjoys the adulation of the fans
Photo by Max Aquino

pg 85: Dallas coach Oscar Pareja
Photo by Matt Warso

Chapter Eleven

Interim Schminterim Brian Schmetzer Hired

By Steven Agen

Steven Agen is the Seattle Editor for Prost Amerika and founder of Radio Cascadia.

The club held its Annual Business Meeting three days after the Dallas home leg. A sea of folding chairs were set out in the cavernous west corridor of CenturyLink Field – Wednesday night or not, it was hardly a surprise that the Front Office had prepared for high demand. The club had acknowledged in the lead up to the meeting that an announcement of some sort would take place. Alliance Council reports and season highlight packages would run their course as usual, but one item on the agenda alone explained the excitement around the event.

The announcement was hardly a secret; what else could it have been? But lack of suspense didn't keep the rave green faithful away. The night wasn't one for surprises, but celebration. The club would publicly recognize what was, frankly, already a foregone conclusion. The fanbase had already been whipped into a frenzy by the first leg of the Conference Semifinals, and the timing of the pre-planned business meeting turned into another moment of serendipity simply too perfect to waste.

We are unlikely to ever find out just what the standard was for Schmetzer to earn the full time job in Seattle. Would he have still gotten it if Real Salt Lake had staged a second half comeback on Decision Day and, coupled with a few other results, Sounders hadn't made the playoffs? What if Ishmael Elfath had sent Alonso off in the Knockout Round, and Sounders succumbed to Benny Feilhaber and Sporting KC? And what if Schmetzer had only watched his side replicate their home leg against Dallas from the 2015 postseason, a narrow 2-1 victory, rather than the 3-0 shellacking they delivered?

This author would argue that Schmetzer got the very best out of the squad that anyone could have in the back half of 2016. Whether individual results at the end of the year went their way or not, he had the team playing at a high enough level that it would have been awfully harsh not to give him a more permanent chance to continue that output.

By stuffing Dallas 3-0 days before the event, it was an utterly moot point. Why even hold the business meeting, if not to confirm what the masses rightly demanded?

On November 2nd, 2016 the Seattle Sounders Front Office formally removed head coach Brian Schmetzer's interim tag.

Brian Schmetzer unveiled as permanent head coach
Photo by Max Aquino

After the side took 20 points from 20 games under Sigi Schmid, Schmetzer led them to an 8-4-2 record through the end of the regular season. The turnaround saw Sounders exactly double their points per game mark, from 1 point per game (PPG) in the first 20 matches to 2 PPG in the last 14. An examination of the Western Conference table offers an equally compelling account of Schmetzer's influence. The 3-0 loss to Sporting KC on July 24 left Sounders 9th in the conference, ten points off of 6th-place Vancouver and the red line. Only three clubs in the league had posted worse records than Seattle through 20 matches.

The ten days leading up to the announcement had seen Schmetzer guide Sounders through must-win games against Real Salt Lake, Sporting KC and FC Dallas – the last of which clearly constituted Sounders' best playoff performance in their MLS history. It had taken Sigi Schmid four seasons to win two playoff games with Seattle, while Schmetzer had reached the mark with his first two cracks at it. After years of playoff futility, the meteorically strong result against Dallas instantly made clear that Sounders had entered a new era in their relationship with the MLS postseason.

That paradigm shift was exactly what many following the club had craved. To be fair, almost every detail regarding Brian Schmetzer was a feather in his cap as it pertained to his coaching credentials.

Local Hero

A graduate of Nathan Hale High School, Schmetzer first suited up for the NASL Sounders in 1980. The team folded in 1983 but the local product had begun his trend of participation in every iteration of the club. In 2002 he took over as head coach of the USL Sounders, leading them to postseason crowns in 2005 and 2007. Those titles were Sounders' first since A-League successes in 1995 and 1996. When the club transitioned to MLS in 2009 Schmetzer became Sigi Schmid's top assistant on the coaching staff. Along with his local roots, his enthusiasm in practice and with the press

quickly made him a favorite in the expansion club as its following grew exponentially from USL days.

Some feared that Schmetzer's long tenure within the club would actually hurt his chances at replacing Schmid. Perhaps Garth Lagerwey, still relatively fresh in Seattle and making his first coaching change, would want to start with a clean slate in 2017 no matter what Schmetzer did. It would not have been outside Lagerwey's rights if he wished to pick his own man for the job rather than potentially compromising for a politically convenient choice.

As a result, when local favorite Schmetzer dropped his interim tag, it felt almost like a trophy for fans to celebrate. However rough the start of the year had been and however the rest of the postseason went, Sounders had accomplished the vital mission of keeping Schmetzer in charge.

While Schmetzer may have seen himself hired even without grand postseason success, there was no harm in trying for it now that Sounders were there. The first leg triumph over Dallas brought with it national recognition as the 3-0 advantage was the largest any club had mustered across four ties. For a club which had been playoff afterthoughts only a week before, common sense now seemed to indicate that Seattle suddenly had as solid a shot at MLS Cup as anyone.

Western Conference Semifinals Leg 2 — FC Dallas 2 : 1 Sounders FC

Sounders recorded their only loss of the 2016 postseason in Texas, but the 2-1 decision meant they advanced comfortably on aggregate.

In his first match as permanent head coach, Schmetzer kept his lineup completely unchanged from the leg in Seattle. Dallas boss Oscar Pareja made two changes and drastically altered the posture of the side from the week before. Mauro Rosales and Tesho Akindele replaced Ryan Hollingshead and Victor Ulloa as Pareja fielded for all the attacking firepower he could find.

The set-up suited Dallas much more than their formation at CenturyLink Field had, and the hosts controlled the early portions of the second leg. However when Frei held a deflected shot from distance off the boot of Figueroa on 14 minutes, it was the closest Dallas would come to a goal before Morris very nearly ended the fixture soon after. He couldn't quite redirect Valdez's deflected cross into the net on the far post, missing inches wide of a quick away goal for Seattle two minutes after Figueroa's effort.

Dallas kept the pressure up and finally found a reward for it 25 minutes into the match. A throw-in from the right side fell for Atiba Harris. He took the ball off of a bounce and crossed first-time from a tight angle near the endline. Pareja's decision to start Akindele looked wise as the forward headed off the underside of the bar and into the net, cutting Sounders' aggregate lead to 3-1. In the moment, the Dallas comeback was perfectly on track as far as timing went. A third of the way into the match, they had a third of the job done.

But realistically, the Shield and Open Cup winners never looked like they'd be able to hold Seattle to zero on the defensive end. From the opening whistle it was apparent that cracks in the Dallas formation, implemented to create an abundance of chances, would yield opportunities for Sounders to kill the game off themselves. Lodeiro hit the inside of the post on a free kick from 30 yards out on 37 minutes. Dallas would fail to threaten again before the break, and at half-time Sounders seemed the more likely to score the next goal.

At 3-1 the job wasn't quite done yet, but 20 solid minutes after Dallas took the lead had calmed nerves and made it clear that Sounders wouldn't face a prolonged lapse like their opponents did the week before.

Half Time — FC Dallas 1 : 0 Sounders FC

Nine minutes after the restart, Tyrone Mears stole the ball off of Walker Zimmerman on the right flank in the attacking third. He picked his head up and sent in a low cross towards three Sounders in the area. An unmarked Lodeiro met it on the edge of the six yard box. Seitz got a hand to his shot, but that hand was not strong enough to keep the ball out. On 54 minutes Sounders had tied the score on the night and led 4-1 on aggregate. Most importantly, their away goal meant that Dallas would need four unanswered scores to put Seattle out of the playoffs. Only utter capitulation would keep Sounders from going through to just their third-ever Conference Final.

Mauro Rosales knocked a cross back towards the center of the area for Urruti on 56 minutes, and Dallas' second headed goal of the night brought the aggregate scoreline to 4-2. The consolation goal brought the crowd back into proceedings, but it was only that – a consolation. Dallas still needed three goals in a half hour to advance. Even in the ascendancy after their second goal, the rescue operation seemed more for show than something built on genuine belief. Sounders saw out the remainder of the game, knocking Dallas out, and sending them through to the Western Conference Finals.

The response to the Dallas goals – not conceding again before the half, staying in the game and creating chances rather than bunkering in, and fully keeping their composure throughout the match – was another convincing demonstration of Sounders' new playoff mentality under Schmetzer. Lodeiro's equalizer was well-earned on the balance of play, but just the fact that Sounders rarely came away with what they felt they'd earned in playoff games under Sigi Schmid highlighted the vastness of the change.

In other words, the first leg was no fluke. Brian Schmetzer may have lost his first match without the interim tag but he showed why it had been removed. Sounders wouldn't need to exclusively rely on eight minute goal barrages to keep advancing. They had pragmatically accomplished this impressive playoff result and proved they could get by on a variety of tactics and styles.

A third Conference Final in eight years was coming to Seattle, and dumping Dallas out of the postseason had the club feeling like anything was possible from there.

Max Aquino
PHOTOGRAPHY
t @maxaquinophoto

The Corporate Overlord You Can Trust

pg 90: Alliance Council President, Stephanie Steiner

pg 91-92: Handshakes & Hugs
Photos by Max Aquino

Chapter Twelve

How The West Was Won

By Richard Fleming

Richard Fleming is a veteran reporter for the BBC and now does match commentary for Western Conference Colorado Rapids

At the end of previous seasons, Seattle fans would be left reflecting upon another campaign in which their team had entertained and frustrated in equal measure. Something, or someone, always seemed to trip them up short of the ultimate goal – from Houston Dynamo in the Western Conference semifinals in their first year (2009) to FC Dallas at the same stage in 2015.

It was intriguing to watch the Sounders from afar in 2016. They had a close-season clear-out heading into the new term, shedding the likes of Chad Barrett, Lamar Neagle, Marco Pappa, Gonzalo Pineda and Andy Rose. The real body-blow, though, came with the late and unexpected departure of star striker Obafemi Martins, a Chinese takeaway who opted for the big bucks on offer at Shanghai Shenhua.

Focus shifted to the old and the new; Clint Dempsey and Jordan Morris. Dempsey, a proven pro, partnering the young gun Morris. The prodigal son had returned, but early signs were one of hype rather than hope.

Offseason upheaval appeared to take its toll, with the Sounders losing their first three games, with two of those reversals coming at

CenturyLink Field, for so long a difficult stop on the MLS road. By the midway stage, the sliding Sounders had gone 5-10-2, suffering as many defeats as they had in all of 2014 en route to the MLS Supporters' Shield.

And their paltry return of just 12 goals meant that, not only were this Sounders side losing games, but they were also failing to entertain their passionate and expectant supporters. There were very few crumbs of comfort.

At this point it is worth noting that no team bottom of the standings at the midway point had ever gone on to make the playoffs, never mind lift MLS Cup. In fact, most of those bottom at the halfway stage would end in that sorry situation, stranded in the gutter, staring up at the stars.

A 5-0 home win over 10-man and depleted FC Dallas in game 18 suggested Sigi Schmid's side may at least drag themselves off the floor of the Western Conference. But successive defeats finally forced ownership to show Schmid the door. With roster change at the start of the season, and now the departure of the only head coach Sounders fans had ever known, 2016 was fast becoming the

Morris, Dempsey and Alonso
Photo by Nick Danielson

worst in franchise history. Never before had they failed to make the playoffs, and never before had they finished lower than fourth.

What made matters worse was that this was the season in which the regular powerhouses were spluttering and stuttering. Portland were weighed heavy by the tag of defending champions, as well as injuries to key components. Sporting Kansas City – champions in 2013 — were inconsistent, while LA Galaxy had finally found out that stars only shine for so long.

Brian Schmetzer, with the look of a university professor, came in as interim head coach on July 26, and a day later the Sounders announced the signing of Nicolás Lodeiro, a Uruguay international from Boca Juniors. The transformation was instant. They went unbeaten in Lodeiro's first five appearances (3-0-2), with the newcomer notching two goals and four assists. From Lodeiro's arrival to the end of the regular season, Seattle went 8-2-4, collecting 28 points from 14 games, at an average of two points per game – exactly double what they had managed from the 20 games previous.

In the early stages of that fine run, and while delicately rebuilding from the rubble of what had become their season, the club was dealt the devastating news that Clint Dempsey had played his last game of the season, due to an irregular heartbeat. In the 10 regular season games missed by Deuce, the Sounders – after a brief period of adjustment – rallied to end the season 5-2-3. More significant is that, against Western Conference playoff rivals, the Sounders were 4-2-3. They were not only adding to their points tally, but they were making dents into the hopes of others.

Now, one will never truly know, but the loss of Dempsey – coupled with the arrival of Lodeiro – appeared to galvanize the side in a way not previously seen. We have grown used to seeing teams built around star names, whereas here was a side – similar to the model made so successful by Caleb Porter at Portland a year

earlier– in which playing as a collective was key, with less reliance on individuals. A case in point was the summer of 2015, when the Sounders went 2-9-0 during a spell when one or more of Osvaldo Alonso, Dempsey and Martins were absent. Lack of talent, meant loss of traction, and highlighted a lack of depth.

But let us not overlook the promotion to interim head coach of the bespectacled Schmetzer. The loyal assistant to Schmid was handed what, at first, appeared a damage-limitation job. It was a season in which expectations had plummeted, disquiet had surfaced at town hall meetings, and the aura around this fascinating franchise had begun to dissipate.

Though, in a sense, the negativity surrounding the Sounders' season may have led, in part, to their resurrection. Being afforded little chance of making anything of the 2016 dumpster fire allowed the Sounders to play with freedom. The shackles were off, from a team that had been written off. The sense of 'we have nothing to lose', coupled with new faces and new ideas in the locker room, provided a platform off which the side would begin their climb.

So often it is stated that 'it's not what you do in the first half of the MLS season which counts, but what you do in the second half'. That may be so, but the Sounders were so shockingly poor over the first 20 games (6-12-2), that a minor miracle were needed. That minor miracle was not one single moment, or one particular person. Lodeiro, Schmetzer, the loss of Dempsey, the injection of confidence, the growth of Morris — all of these elements contributed to the mountain not only being climbed, but ultimately conquered.

Momentum is a magical thing. As results began to turn back in favor of the Sounders, the Rave Green became a team few fancied facing. They had their swagger back. The fans sensed something special, and the national narrative was one of 'could they do the unthinkable?'.

As a then 27-year-old, Nicolás Lodeiro was not only talented, but he was one of a new wave of Designated Players landing in the league who were still in their prime. He, as well as 28-year-old Shkëlzen Gashi at the Colorado Rapids, were two examples of a shift in the gaze of those seeking talent.

MLS supporters have a knowledge of the global game that should not be underestimated. They have access to live soccer from the world's leading leagues, and are far more educated on which players would be a decent fit for their club than many would give them credit. Plus, in the modern age of the world-wide web, information is just a mouse click away.

Fans these days still want to watch household names, but they are also more demanding of those players. Selling jerseys is one thing, but there is now a greater emphasis on there being a return on the field as well. Lodeiro may not have fallen into the Kaka, Gerrard or Lampard category of soccer superstars, but the Sounders' faithful swiftly took him to their hearts as he was able to do what the fans demanded of him. Selling jerseys and getting TV eyeballs on the big names is, of course, needed in a growing league. For the fans, though, the priority has shifted. No longer is it a case of 'have I heard of him?', rather the requirement is a much more simple 'can he play?'. And Lodeiro could.

So, having surged into the playoffs, the Sounders then edged Sporting Kansas City through an 88th minute winner from Nelson Valdez, before hitting an FC Dallas machine which had run out of steam. LA Galaxy, meanwhile, ran out of luck in a penalty shootout loss to the Colorado Rapids.

Against the Rapids in the Western Conference Championship, the Sounders managed to do what no other team had achieved in 2016 – beat Colorado in Colorado, 1-0, for a 3-1 aggregate victory. In both games against the Rapids, local lad Jordan Morris added to the 12 goals he had notched during the regular season. The bulk of his goals came in the first half of the year, suggesting others were prepared to shoulder the work-load as the need for success heightened – another sign of a more balanced unit.

Seattle showed in the second half of 2016 that they were the most consistent team in MLS. To achieve that, you need ability, and yet the only real addition of note during the campaign was that of Lodeiro. In other words, the Sounders had ability throughout the year, but ability will only serve you so well. Even the elite athletes need a significant sprinkling of belief, confidence and direction.

In what was a season of two halves, the Sounders were the ageing prize-fighter being picked on and poked fun at by those that had once cowered. The get-up-and-go had got up and gone. Top-level sport is often won and lost on margins. Not too much changed – a new head coach here, a talented Designated Player there – but it proved enough for Seattle Sounders FC to remember who they were, and what they were capable of, thereby triggering the greatest comeback in MLS history.

Chapter Thirteen

Sounders Reach New Heights at Altitude

By Steven Agen

Steven Agen is the Seattle Editor for Prost Amerika and founder of Radio Cascadia.

Rapids — Masters of the close game

The Colorado Rapids made their living in 2016 on games decided by a single goal.

Eight of their 15 wins on the season were 1-0 results. A 3-1 decision against Seattle on April 23 and a 2-0 win over Vancouver on August 6 were, remarkably, their only multi-goal wins of the season. However, they were shut out only eight times in 34 league games.

The Rapids only lost by a 1-0 scoreline only twice, demonstrating their control in tight matches. An 8-2 record in such affairs was good for the top mark in the league. Given that they only lost by multiple goals twice as well, 30 of their matches were decided by one goal or fewer and they took at least a draw in 26 of them. They played solid defense, giving up only 32 goals all season. For team that had missed the playoffs in 2015, their consistency throughout the campaign was truly something to marvel at.

The stats painted the portrait of a Rapids side making their living off of keeping clean sheets and making single goal leads count. The roster was aptly built for such a style, centered on summer acquisition USMNT goalkeeper Tim Howard, another USMNT star midfield engine Jermaine Jones and an array of noteworthy attackers including former EPL striker Kevin Doyle and leading goalscorer Shkelzen Gashi.

Their efforts had rewarded them with the 2nd seed in the Western Conference and a bye through the Knockout Round after taking 58 points on a 15-13-6 record. Their qualification for the Conference Championship came by virtue of a penalty shootout win over the LA Galaxy. To absolutely no-one's surprise, the clubs had split two 1-0 results and were level on aggregate after 180 minutes. Gashi's screamer from distance tied the series up on 36 minutes in the second leg, canceling out Giovani dos Santos' first leg tally. Half an hour of extra time could not separate the teams either.

It was dos Santos who would go on to miss a spot kick in the shootout before Howard saved two more himself, putting the Rapids through 1-1 on aggregate, 3-1 on penalties. The one-goal game style worked, as the Rapids were headed to their first Conference Championship since their run to MLS Cup in 2010.

Colorado Rapids coach, Pablo Mastroeni
Photo by Corbin Elliott

Avoiding Arena

From Sounders' perspective, the postseason had finally progressed far enough such that title credentials were to based off of playoff form rather than seeding. The 2-1 loss in Dallas had done little to quell the national interest in Seattle's first dalliance with MLS Cup in several years' time, and Colorado's utilitarian style didn't dominate anyone's attention the way the Texans had.

Colorado advancing past LA had suited Seattle just fine. Bruce Arena's mastery of playoff soccer had knocked Sounders out of both previous Conference Championships they participated in (2012 & 2014). The Galaxy possessed more high profile attacking talents than the Rapids and also carried the distinction of being the most successful club in MLS playoff history. The Rapids were not to be taken lightly, drab countenance or otherwise, but playing a Conference Championship series against someone other than postseason bogey team LA was a reason in itself to get excited for the prospect of a first MLS Cup appearance.

Sounders' history with Colorado was reason for optimism as well. Their only prior postseason meeting was a 2-0 Seattle win in the 2013 Knockout Round, with Brad Evans and Eddie Johnson providing the goals on the night when goalkeeper Michael Gspurning was sent off late for an odd handball outside the area.

The Rapids had beaten Sounders at CenturyLink Field earlier in 2016, but it was before Lodeiro's arrival or Schmetzer's promotion. Most importantly, it was the only the second time Colorado had ever won at Seattle in MLS play. Including their playoff match in 2013, Sounders held a dominant 9-1-2 record at home against Colorado. A road record of 5-1-2 in Commerce City, Colorado was nothing scoff at either, particularly compared to the alternative. Seattle's track record when playing at LA included only one victory at the time.

16 days and an international break separated the Colorado series from the one with Dallas. The gap was a huge boon for a Sounders squad on the older side, but held another surprise offering for Seattle beyond the time to rest up. Tim Howard had picked up a broken adductor bone while playing with the US men's national team in a World Cup Qualifier against Mexico. The leader of the Rapids' backline, only freshly settled in from his move over to the club from Everton, was done for the season.

While he underwent surgery to repair the fracture, backup Zac MacMath readied himself for the two biggest matches of his life. The former Philadelphia Union goalkeeper had lost the 2014 US Open Cup final to Sounders already, and surely wouldn't want to repeat the experience in the 2016 postseason. No amount of preparation from the 25 year old could solve the problem, though losing Howard a week before the Conference Championship was a huge blow.

Western Conference Championship, 1st Leg Sounders FC 2 : 1 Colorado Rapids

Most of the 42,774 rain gear-clad supporters at CenturyLink Field, braving the elements in a rare November home game, stood for the duration of the Tuesday contest in recognition of its importance. The fierce weather could not dampen their voices. The electricity before kickoff was something that everyone in attendance will never forget, even for those with standards raised by years of brilliant displays of fan pageantry in Cascadia. It was only their third opportunity to play a part in sending their club through to MLS Cup for the first time, and the other two hadn't gone well. Their hunger lingered palpably in the air.

Roman Torres replaced Zach Scott at center back as Schmetzer's only change from the lineup that had ended Dallas' interest little more than two weeks before. Nelson Valdez started as the lone striker again, having nearly scored a header in a third consecutive playoff match when he nodded a Lodeiro free kick just wide on 50 minutes in Frisco. MacMath replacing Howard accounted for Colorado head coach Pablo Mastroeni's only change from their second leg win over LA.

The Rapids' record in one-goal games was no mystery, and as a result common sense held that Sounders could use the first leg drastically increase their odds of advancing in two ways: by scoring the first goal in the series, and by not conceding an away goal. The former would keep Seattle from becoming Colorado's ninth 1-0 win of the season and the latter would give them a huge advantage down the road if the series was close.

That plan was quickly upended when Kevin Doyle scored with the first chance of the game after a tense opening twelve and a half minutes. Gashi dummied a Jones pass for Doyle to run onto at the top of the box, and his shot deflected off Chad Marshall and looped into the net. The touch off the center back removed Frei from the equation, and he could only watch as the ball sailed in and the Rapids celebrated their early away goal.

It was the sort of freak play that seemed to plague Sounders earlier in the season, an affliction which disappeared as quickly as it had arrived once Schmetzer righted the ship. The team had a habit of responding poorly to difficult situations akin to this one earlier in the season, and this was now ostensibly an uphill battle for the rest of the series. Sounders would have to beat the Rapids at their own game now.

Looking back at it, the moments after the Rapids took the lead were likely the most difficult, uncertain minutes of the entire Seattle postseason. The visitors had done exactly the thing they needed to do to make the entire series a very unpleasant proposition for Sounders. Who knows how long those in and around the club would have dwelled in that malcontent headspace, if Jordan Morris had not equalized at first opportunity six minutes later. Maybe a

stingy Rapids defense would have lived up to their reputation and clung to their goal advantage all the way through the end of the second leg. We can certainly say that the longer it would have gone on at 1-0, the more dire it would have gotten for Sounders.

But Nicolas Lodeiro flicked a pass into the path of Cristian Roldan near midfield, and Roldan settled the ball in his stride after touching it down with his head. The ball sat nicely for him and he laced a shot from distance. It struck the inside of the post but bounced out. However Jordan Morris did react before anyone else, and he did beat MacMath with his rebound effort, and the Seattle Sounders were level just six minutes after conceding to stingy Colorado. The away goal was still a factor, but knocking the Rapids' advantage down to just a tiebreaker meant Doyle's strike had a fraction of the value it did before the 19th minute.

In a postseason that also included Valdez's header against Sporting KC and the eight minute burst against Dallas, Morris' goal stands out as the single brightest example of resolve and character embodied by Schmetzer's playoff Sounders. They had a mountain to climb, and they did it quickly. The goal itself featured ingenuity from Lodeiro, maturity and confidence from Roldan, and poacher's instinct from Morris. Their most difficult moment brought out their best, and did so when they needed it the most.

MacMath probably should have done better with Roldan's initial strike than he did, but he soon made up for it with two important stops in the 31st minute. Erik Friberg crossed from the endline and hit an open Lodeiro, who generated as much pace as he could on his header from twelve yards out only to see MacMath palm the ball behind for a corner. It was Lodeiro's turn to cross after Sounders took a short set piece, and Valdez forced MacMath into an even better save off a right footed shot from the edge of the six yard box. Only MacMath's point-blank reaction kept the Rapids from a 2-1 half-time deficit.

Aside from two botched one-on-one chances from former Sounder Sebastien Le Toux, one on either side of half-time, Sounders were firing on all cylinders and dictating tempo for most of the last seventy minutes. It was no more than Seattle deserved when Lodeiro earned a penalty off another former Sounder, Marc Burch, on the hour mark. The left back knocked Lodeiro down as the playmaker ran away from goal. The Uruguayan stepped up to take the penalty himself and converted for his fourth goal of the postseason. Sounders had turned the series around, and led 2-1 with exactly two thirds of it left to play.

Rapids captain Sam Cronin received a yellow card in the 67th minute, leaving him suspended for the second leg. It was a heavy additional blow for Mastroeni beyond the goal disadvantage and the absence of Howard as he surely already started to ponder the return leg.

Lodeiro would go on to curl just over the bar from acres of space on the edge of the area on 76 minutes, the last clear chance for either side. A third goal wouldn't present itself before the end of the ninety minutes, but Sounders were good value for their lead. The result could be met with even more optimism when remembering that Colorado scored first. Previous Conference Championship first legs had both ended in defeat, and that alone made 2-1 an excellent result for both the team and its fans. Seattle were ninety more minutes away from MLS Cup.

Western Conference Championships, 2nd Leg — Colorado Rapids 0 : 1 Sounders FC

A strong Seattle away contingent made its presence known from and hour and a half before kickoff, flags flapping vigorously on a windy afternoon at Dick's Sporting Goods Park. 17,695 eventually piled in to see who would represent the Western Conference in the league's showpiece event. Another tight, tense game was expected.

A 0-0 draw would put Seattle through, but a 1-0 home win would see Colorado advance on away goals.

Only five days separated the two matches of the Western Conference Championships, prompting rest issues for an older Sounders squad that was rapidly draining the energy their veterans had left. Erik Friberg dropped to the bench in favor of Andreas Ivanschitz making Sounders' sole change from the first leg. Plenty of other tired legs stayed in the starting eleven though, many running on grit and adrenaline by the time the team got to Commerce City, Rapids' Colorado home.

Mastroeni tinkered with his lineup for the second leg beyond swapping out the suspended Cronin. Jermaine Jones pushed into the center of the midfield band of three with Michael Azira and Dillon Powers behind him. The role gave the former Schalke man greater flexibility in the attack and fewer responsibilities on the other end. Dominique Badji moved to the bench and Kevin Doyle took his place up top to complete the shakeup.

The Rapids started well, pressing forward with attacking flair unseen in the first leg. Jermaine Jones appeared to have an open look at goal on a 6th minute set piece, but he couldn't make solid contact with his header. The hosts were clearly in control, but even their style upgrade hadn't yet seen them create enough goal-dangerous moments.

Frei and Torres suffered a miscommunication on 23 minutes, with Doyle slipping in between them on the left edge of the box. The Irishman's cross past an empty net did not however connect with another Rapid. Jones poked the ball just over the net after Frei didn't get the most convincing of touches on the ensuing corner. The goalkeeper would still have been out of his net if Jones had been able to put the ball on target through a narrow window.

Miscommunication aside, Sounders sat in and absorbed pressure well in the first half. They didn't show much ambition going forward, but had neutralized a Colorado attack that looked totally revamped from five days before. Jones continued to be involved in everything going forward for the Rapids, pulling the strings from the middle of the park. However he couldn't lead them past the suddenly stingy Sounders defense to a breakthrough before half-time. The hosts dominated the possession and shot statistics, but failed to put a single one on target. Nobody was comfortable on a bitterly cold day in Colorado but Sounders had been given little to deal with given the circumstances.

The theme would continue in the second half, where Seattle would also start to find a bit more space on the counter. The Rapids looked out of ideas and the feeling that Sounders were in control grew stronger. On 56 minutes Morris, battling a flu virus he'd picked up in the days after the first leg, collected a through ball from Nelson Valdez and chipped it over an onrushing Zac MacMath and into the net. All the Rapids possession, shots and corner were for nought. Jordan Morris had just put Seattle ahead before Colorado could record a shot on goal.

Three Sounders subbed off with various injuries in the second half, but they held on firm to their two goal advantage. Most concerningly, Osvaldo Alonso departed with a painful knee injury that threatened to keep him out of any potential cup finals. But the Rapids would never go on to record that elusive first shot on goal, and Alonso popped up off the bench and celebrated with his teammates as the full-time whistle sounded. Seattle had built up a head of steam that the Rapids, admittedly uninspired over both legs, could never counter. From 19 minutes into the first leg on, Sounders were almost flawless.

The team ran over to the away contingent in the corner, and then back to midfield to receive the Western Conference Championship trophy. The silverware was quickly whisked back over towards the

travelling support after a quick photo shoot. As the home fans filed out of the stadium, Sounders' one packed section stayed and rejoiced with the players, and all the rest of the Seattle soccer community with them.

pg 106: Jermaine Jones holds off Mears and Torres

pg 107: Morris outjumps four Rapids defenders
Photos by Corbin Elliott

Chapter Fourteen

Stefan Frei
From Toronto to Toronto

By Matt Pentz

Matt Pentz is a freelance soccer journalist who writes for the Guardian, ESPNFC, yahoo.com and weekly on the Sounders FC on Prost Amerika.

The day of the MLS Cup final began inauspiciously for Sounders goalkeeper Stefan Frei.

He awoke that morning to news that his mother Marlies was being prevented from boarding her Toronto-bound flight at San Francisco international airport. A native of Switzerland, Frei's mother hadn't applied for the travel visas she'd needed in time.
She frantically called both of her sons in a panic, but there was nothing to be done – she would have to watch the biggest match of Stefan's life from afar.

For the keeper, it was just one more distraction in a fortnight full of them.

Seattle's matchup with Toronto was unfortunate for a number of reasons. First and foremost, it meant the championship game would be played at BMO Field instead of CenturyLink. Had Montreal triumphed over their Canadian rivals, Sounders would have had home advantage in the final.

It also meant that Frei, who spent five seasons with TFC before an unceremonious trade to the Sounders in late 2013, would

spend much of the two-week build-up in the media spotlight as an obvious major storyline. And that came without even delving into the unresolved emotional baggage Frei carried with him on his return to his former home city.

This was one bridge too far. He turned to his older brother Michael and asked him to deal with their mother. Stefan rolled back over on his bed at the team hotel and resumed fitfully visualizing what he hopes will be a triumphant night.

"Mom can get a little crazy," Stefan said. "'You deal with it. I've got a game to play in a few hours.'"

Boy, did he.

Advantage Canada?

Most objective observers would have given Toronto FC a slight edge heading into the title game.

Toronto was playing at home. They were still glowing with the positive vibes from that epic conference final series against

A keeper's best friend? Stefan Frei kisses the goal post
Photo by Brandon Bleek

Montreal. Sebastian Giovinco might not have won his second straight MLS Most Valuable Player award, but he was still the consensus best player in the league among his peers. U.S. men's national team stalwarts Michael Bradley and Jozy Altidore were playing well and keenly focused on the task at hand.

Oddsmakers would have been even more bullish on TFC had they been given a glimpse behind Seattle's closed locker room doors.

The Sounders drove themselves down to the nub in turning what was once a 10-point deficit in the playoff hunt into an unlikely Western Conference championship. Star rookie Jordan Morris, who shrugged off the stomach flu to score the goal that booked their place in MLS Cup in Colorado, was dealing with a muscle injury. Veteran winger Andreas Ivanschitz was moving around gingerly too. Both starting center backs, Chad Marshall and Roman Torres, were severely banged up.

Midfield anchor Osvaldo Alonso, according to former Seattle assistant Ante Razov, "probably shouldn't have even been on the field."

"When you push guys that hard, when for your last 15 games, every one is a must-win game, it's pretty ridiculous," Razov said.

It wasn't as though the Sounders were even playing all that well. The 8-2-4 record with which they closed the regular season speaks for itself but they weren't exactly playing flashy soccer – they were very direct and very predictable, if not easy to actually stop.

During the brief window in which summer signing Nicolas Lodeiro and Clint Dempsey played alongside each other, Seattle's attack looked as fearsome as any in the league. After Dempsey was ruled out for the season, however, it was forced to adjust.

Coach Brian Schmetzer, who took over on an interim basis from Sigi Schmid in late July, installed a 4-2-3-1 formation that prized solidity over style. With Dempsey down, the team congealed around defensive midfielders Alonso and Cristian Roldan. They patrolled in front of a reliable back four, Seattle made itself hard to break down and Lodeiro and Morris made just enough plays to push the team over the line.

With the exception of a blockbuster second half spell against FC Dallas which produced three goals in eight minutes in the conference semifinals, the Sounders barely managed to survive from round to round.

A pair of controversial offside calls – one that penalized Sporting Kansas and the flag that stayed down during Nelson Valdez's late game-winner – were required to see off Sporting in a one-game playoff. Alonso, too, was fortunate not to have seen a second yellow card and an ejection early in the second half.

Colorado looked set to take command of that Western Conference finals series before Morris struck on the counter.

"I can't even say it was anything we particular that we did on the field," former Sounders forward Herculez Gomez said. "We didn't do anything particularly well. We were like the Bad News Bears. But we had the momentum, and it was an individual act of brilliance here and there, or 20 minutes of collective effort, and it snowballed. We turned into this machine that nobody wanted to play."

In some sense, the Sounders became so inured to adversity that they came to thrive on it. Having lost influential forward Obafemi Martins to the Chinese Super League so close to the beginning of the season, coach Sigi Schmid to a bad run of form and Dempsey to that irregular heartbeat, this team had no choice but to learn how to roll with the punches.

By the time they landed in Toronto the week of MLS Cup, there was a quiet confidence within the squad that if all those previous breaks hadn't stopped them then, nothing was going to now. There was also a sense things were finally going their way, perhaps bordering on a feeling of inevitability

"This sounds cheesy, but it was something that was meant to be," Gomez said. "... It felt like this team was supposed to be in the final."

The coldest of warm-ups

The official temperature at kickoff of the final was recorded at 28 degrees Fahrenheit, or negative 2.22 in the Celsius of the host nation. Those numbers do little to give you a full sense of just how damn cold it was that night in Toronto.

BMO Field sits on the shores of Lake Ontario, and the wind whipped in frigid sweeps off the water. Prior to the pregame build-up and at half-time, bundled-up fans gathered beneath the heat lamps lining the concourses to thaw out.

Just how cold was it? When the BMO groundskeepers watered the field before warmups in accordance with league rules, the ball started to pick up ice. For Frei and the Sounders goalkeepers, the flying orb resembled a snowball as they were peppered with practice shots.

"His warmup was terrible," said Seattle goalkeeping coach Tom Dutra, who tried to keep a mounting sense of panic to himself. "It was like catching an ice cube. 'Rub your gloves on your beard. Get the gristle going.'"

Run back the video of the final, and you'll see evidence of this: Frei frantically scrubbing his paws on his facial hair to scrape off the ice that accumulated on his gloves, like a man trying to banish a particularly troubling thought. Ice gathered on the posts and crossbars too. Frei could even feel the uneven ridges when he leaned on the post to set up his defensive wall prior to an early Toronto free kick.

"It would have been awesome if someone would have pinged the crossbar," Frei said. "Ice would have shattered everywhere."

Something else happened during warmups that would ultimately shape the course of the final. Though most goalkeepers do their best not to show it, they can very much hear the fans packed behind their goal. Frei even has an internal, running list of the most creative (Kansas City, Portland) and nastiest (Salt Lake) hecklers in the league.

So though he appeared to be locked into his pregame drills, Frei was very much aware of the taunts being hurled in his direction by the Toronto fans packed into the beer garden behind the goal.

"I heard fans behind me yelling stupid stuff, and I turned around, and they were all really young fans," said Frei, and notably not the same diehards who had been so supportive throughout his time in Toronto. "It made me feel disconnected, which was a good thing. This is a new generation. They're just fans, and I'm just the away goalkeeper."

Suddenly, some of the conflicting emotions he'd brought into his return as the prodigal son vanished.

"They were trying to dig stuff up – 'I know where your wife Jennifer lives,' and stuff like that – but it almost made me feel good," Frei said. "Feelings would have been stranger if someone behind the goal had been yelling, 'Stefan, we miss you. You're still the best.'"

Frei rebuilds his career and confidence in Seattle

Even more than four years removed from his departure, it's hard for Frei to sum up his time in Toronto in just a few words.

TFC gave him his start as a first-round draft pick out of the University of California. It's the city where he came of age, where he found himself during those formative early-20s. Toronto is where Frei met his future wife, at a Halloween party for which he was dressed as the Incredible Hulk and she in plain clothes having just gotten off a long flight.

"We still have a place there," Frei said. "It's where our two kids – our two dogs – joined us. There are so many good memories, we have so many friends that we still have there."

Yet Toronto is also where Frei spent the darkest portion of his career, where he asked serious questions about his future and whether he was cut out to be a professional soccer player, after all.

The first blow came early in 2012, when Frei suffered a broken fibula in training that would ultimately cost him that entire year. When it first happened, he approached his rehab with characteristic gusto. The process was long and grueling, so comprehensive that to start, he had to re-teach himself how to walk. It was Frei's first serious injury, and even if he mostly put on a brave face, there were moments when he doubted himself.

"You know how things are supposed to be done, but your body is just not willing to do it," Frei said. "Then, it's, 'Can I not do it anymore or am I just not there yet?' It can be difficult. You can kill yourself over it, and think that, no, you just can't do it anymore. And you'll never get out of that hole."

He dragged himself back out. Frei approached 2013 with fresh enthusiasm. With so much time spent in the gym, he was as fit as

he'd been in his entire life, and he looked forward to winning back his starting spot.

Then 44 minutes into his first preseason game, charging out to clear a bouncing ball with a header, Ryan Finley, a rookie on trial with the opposing Crew caught him flush in the face with a high boot. That collision broke Frei's nose, required surgery and cost him another few months.

"That messed me up big time," Frei said. "Because I'm a firm believer that you get out what you put in. You work your butt off for a year, and you expect to be rewarded."

That reward does not typically include literal kicks to the face. Frei's confidence in both his body and ability were shot. The timing could hardly have been worse – he was coming to the end of his contract – and he requested sessions with TFC's sports psychologists to deal with the stress.

Badly in need of a blank slate, the trade to the Sounders in December of 2013 was a godsend. The pittance of a conditional draft pick for which Frei was dealt speaks to just how far his stock fallen both with Toronto and around the league.

Seattle's attacking firepower provided cover while Frei regained confidence and gave the coaching staff the leeway to stick with him. Despite some early shakiness from their custodian, the Sounders opened the 2014 season near the top of the Supporters' Shield standings and stayed there.

Frei recognized the contribution his forwards made to buying him the time he needed.

"It is business," Frei said. "If I make a mistake and lose 1-0, you have to make a change. But if I make a mistake and we win 2-1, it allows them to keep that confidence. It gave me the time to allow me to grow again."

Still, the patience of even the most benevolent of leaders has a limit. In the aftermath of a 2-2 draw in Vancouver late that May, Frei was certain that he had reached it.
Midway through the first half, he charged heedlessly out of his own penalty box to collect a pass from teammate Marco Pappa. Despite being under very little pressure, Frei flubbed his attempted clearance right into the heart of Vancouver's attack. With the goalkeeper on an island, Whitecaps midfielder Gershon Koffie calmly lobbed a soft shot over Frei's net into an empty net.

"I looked like a dum-dum," Frei said.

Even though the Sounders rallied to save a point, Frei spent the weekend in a state of anxiety. Few athletes are as self-flagellating as goalkeepers. This one spent days replaying his latest mistake in his mind, dreading the moment it'll get run back for real in front of his teammates.

"Goalkeepers always know when they messed up," Frei said. "There could be a guy scoring a worldie, and you're still going to be self-critical and wonder what you could have done differently."

When Schmid turns to him that Monday turning film-study, Frei thinks he knows what's coming. He does not. Frei quoted Schmid's words.

"'Don't sweat it. We've got you,' the coach told me. "I remember driving home from that meeting and having the biggest smile on my face. And then I'd show up the next day for work all excited, and that's how I improved, from the inside.

"Sigi saw something in me when people and even I almost doubted myself."

There were other markers along the way but that was the moment, Frei says. That was the exchange that would ultimately turn a broken goalkeeper into the one who would take his place between the sticks on a fateful December night in Toronto.
He came a long way from Point A to B. Seattle won both the U.S. Open Cup and regular-season titles in 2014, Frei making key saves down the stretch as it falls just one goal shy of the league title games.

The 2015 season is probably Frei's best as a pro. And by the time of the dramatic 2016 playoff run, Frei is rightly regarded as one of the very best goalkeepers in MLS, capable of reaching heights that could single-handedly change even the biggest of matches. All of that, he brings with him to Toronto and the league title game.

"I knew he had the ability to have that kind of game," Dutra said. "Whether he could control the emotions, that, I didn't know. I just didn't know – going back to the team that got rid of him; his wife's family is from there; he still owns a place there. All of these things, plus the media demands.

"I knew everything else was going to be fine, but I wasn't sure emotionally how everything was going to affect him."

The save that broke Toronto's spirit

There is something storybook about Schmetzer being the coach to finally bring MLS Cup to his hometown club.

This has been his team since he was signed fresh of out of Nathan Hale High in 1980, so young that his father, Walter, had to co-sign the contract for his underage son. Schmetzer's career path is the story of Seattle soccer, from the North American Soccer League through the indoor and minor leagues that kept the flame of the game alive in the city until MLS arrived in 2009.

Spare a thought for Schmid, though, who toiled for more than seven years toward this elusive accomplishment and had to watch it come to fruition from a broadcast booth rather than the sidelines. This is his night, too – the hand he played in the rebirth of the player who would be named MVP is just one particularly illustrative example of many.

Down below Schmid, the game that unfolds is cautious and hotly contested. Finals are often like this, the pressure snuffing out creativity, necessitating the type of match later recalled fondly only by the winner.

The Sounders sat deep, Alonso and Roldan patrolling aggressively in front of a solid defensive four. Dempsey practiced with the team the morning before at BMO Field, inspiring fleeting hopes of a dramatic comeback, but it wasn't to be. With him out and Morris hampered by injury, they attacked disjointedly if at all. Seattle would ultimately set an infamous MLS Cup record as the first finalist not to record a single shot on goal.

"We weren't bothered by that," Razov said. "We knew we had banged up guys on the field. They probably shouldn't have been out there. But it was a championship. They laid it out there. In any championship, no matter how good you are, you have to have some luck. We had luck."

They had luck – and they had Frei. The Sounders goalkeeper was tested early and often, which kept the blood moving through his numb limbs, if nothing else.

Altidore rolled a shot inches wide of the right post less than two minutes in. Giovinco sliced his effort into the side netting with a clean look on goal early in the second half. The shutout held through 45 minutes, 60 minutes, 90.

Altidore looked poised to win it in stoppage time, when a late corner kick bounced toward him alone at the back post, but Frei cleared the ball away with a flailing punch. The powerful American forward was denied even more improbably midway through extra time via the iconic moment of this championship game. In the 108th minute of a scoreless match, Toronto substitute Tosaint Ricketts pushed forward up the right wing. Making a rare miscalculation, an exhausted Torres dives at Ricketts' feet but failed to knock the ball away, giving the TFC man plenty of time to pick out his cross.

The ball floated, almost lazily, toward the penalty spot, where Altidore was waiting. Arching his back like a leaping salmon, the forward headed it toward the top corner. Altidore later admitted that he was certain his shot was heading in.

To judge by their faces, the home fans whose taunts from the same beer garden had so motivated Frei, thought it was the title-winner, too.

Yet Frei's reaction was immediate. He chopped his feet, gathered himself, threw his body backwards and to his left. Just when all looked to be lost, he reached out with a desperate glove to flick the ball wide of the far post.

The setback appeared to exhaust Toronto's fighting spirit. From then on, the game looked destined for the penalty-shootout tiebreaker.

The Penalties

Altidore scores his for the hosts, as does Brad Evans for the Sounders. Toronto misses, Seattle makes; Toronto makes, Seattle misses. Four consecutive conversions take us into the sudden death round, where TFC's Justin Morrow leaves the door open for Torres to deliver the title.

Stefan Frei organizes his defense
Photo by Lyndsay Radnedge

The muscular Panamanian fires his shot into the back of the net then wheels away in triumph. His teammates chase him around the field in front of a stadium shocked into silence, their faces feral with pure glee.

Homecoming Heroes

The visiting locker room afterward was a whirlwind spitting Heineken and Champagne. Happy bodies dance in the middle in a solid mass, an occasional player getting pulled out for postgame media duties.

Frei himself doesn't get back to the team hotel until 2 a.m., where fans remain waiting to greet their hero despite the late hour. Seattle owner Adrian Hanauer had booked a conference room for the players and their families and friends. The bar at their impromptu party shut down at 3, giving Frei little time to drink in the championship.

"The adrenaline was still so high," Frei said. "I think that's when you started doubting whether it had really happened or not. When you were on the field and saw the confetti and got your metal and saw the happy faces, that was almost comforting. It did really happen. Now, all of a sudden you're in a room where everybody is civil again, it's, 'Did that just happen?'"

His wife pulled up the video clip on her phone, providing him a first glimpse at the replay of his save, which he still hadn't seen. He would spend the following Monday frantically scrolling through his Twitter feed, his mentions filling up so quickly that his thumb could never reach the top.

There were videos of his save in different languages, and all kinds of various memes. His brother forwarded along the reaction from their native Switzerland.

"Well, alright, I guess (the save) was decent,'" Frei says with typical Swiss understatement.

The MLS offseason arrived mercilessly for its reigning champs.

The morning after the title game, as early as 8 a.m. – alternatively, five hours after their bartenders stopped serving drinks—the front office sat players down for exit interviews. More than a couple of them were informed that they wouldn't be back for 2017. 13 Sounders, many of whom played vital roles in the championship run, had their contact options declined within the first few days of the title game.

Hanauer wanted to fly all of his charges somewhere after the parade that Tuesday in downtown Seattle, but the squad broke up quickly.

"We had people from all over the world," Frei notes, passing along the popular sentiment. "I want to get the hell out of here. I want to go home. It's been an eleven-month season. I'm done."

In contrast to, say, the Cleveland Cavaliers, many of whom were photographed shirtless in Las Vegas in the hours following their dramatic NBA championship win, Sounder celebrations were comparatively tame. The flight back from Colorado and the Western Conference final was actually more raucous, when that afternoon kickoff allowed for a livelier evening. The trip back to Toronto was quieter, content.

"In retrospect, instead of going from Toronto to Seattle, we should have gone Toronto, Vegas for 24 hours – chill at every dance club we can find with the shirt on our backs and nothing else – and then come back to Seattle," Frei said. "I guess we'll just have to win another one."

The goalkeeper and his coach didn't get a chance to decompress until a few weeks later, when both were back in Seattle for Christmas Eve. Dutra and his wife hosted Frei and his, chatting about everything but soccer.

Dutra pulled Frei aside for a quick, private moment to tell him how proud he was – a moment just as swiftly broken up by a fresh wave of holiday revelers.

Word travels fast in the suburb of Issaquah. Before long, the entire neighborhood becomes aware that the MLS Cup MVP is in their midst. Holiday spirit inspires extra generosity.

"All of a sudden I've got like six neighbors coming over, offering me wine," Dutra said. "And I know it's because they wanted to see Stef. That was the real reason.

"Stef doesn't like all attention. ... He's just kind of like, 'Thanks.'" He's humble and gracious."

Mostly, the goalkeeper sat back and marveled at how far he'd come in just a few weeks. He'd woken up the morning of the title game to a panicky call from his mother and gone to bed that night a champion.

Stefan Frei might have been an unlikely hero, but that fitted with the overall theme of this Sounders season, of all seasons. Adversity made all of them stronger, and it pushed them over the edge to accomplish what had long eluded the club.

The day of MLS Cup began inauspiciously for Frei, yet that might have been as good a sign as any.

pg 118: Swiss yell or is it a yodel?
Photo by Matt Warso

pg 119: Hard day's work. Frei returns to the locker room
Photo by Nick Danielson

Chapter Fifteen
Watching the Horror Unfold

By Ed Pham

Ed Pham is a Seattle-based Timbers fan who was hoping for a lifetime of insufferable gloating. Now he wishes he hadn't paced himself.

"Fuck, did he really just do that?"

Those were the words that came out my mouth the moment that a certain Stefan Frei made one of the most ridiculous saves I had seen in all my involvement playing or watching soccer. I was at my computer at my apartment and I could see the posts on Facebook at the sheer amazement and heard the cheers coming from the neighborhood at the same moment. For me, that wasn't the case. I was just sitting glaring at the screen.

See, I'm a Timbers fan...that lives in Seattle.

The night that the Portland Timbers won the cup, I posted a photo of me holding the MLS Cup. It was a momentous occasion for me because not only did the Timbers win it all, but I could show off that photo to all Sounders folks I knew up in Seattle. After all the flak I had received for the US Open Cups that Sounders had to the Timbers' zero, it was the one photo I could show rival fans and tell them, "Well, we won a MLS Cup" and they would just walk away grumbling.

It wasn't just me. There is a group of us Timbers fans who live in Seattle that reveled in the fact that our team had the MLS Cup and Sounders had not. For some of us, we would hang our Timbers scarves in cubicles or office windows with such pride because of that victory, only to get glares from co-workers that were Sounders fans. Many in our group got into some friendly banter with other Sounders friends and family. I remember going to one of my rec soccer team's games soon after that Sunday and just yelling, "MLS Champions!" as I saw them all. A couple congratulated me. Most just ignore me or said, "Whatever, Ed." Those couple of months in the offseason were just a grand time for all of myself and the rest of us Timbers fans.

We thought it would last forever.

Sounders' 2016 season was pretty poor to start. No Obafemi Martins for Sounders meant they were struggling without their talisman attacker. Timbers were struggling as well. The regular season is a marathon though, not a sprint. It's what happens at the end of the season that matters most. That's what I learned last year during the Timbers' run to hoisting the MLS Cup. I'd have some banter with a co-worker about how Sounders were doing.

Portland's Jack Jewsbury watches Lodeiro in a derby
Photo by Diego Diaz

Sometimes, I'd pretend to knock over her Zach Scott bobblehead doll, because I am THAT brave when he's nowhere to be seen. Midway through the season, Sigi was frustrating her. I said, "Maybe they'll just see him out in order to respect him for the work he's done." I figured they'd stick with him until the end of the season at least.

Then Sounders fired Sigi after Sounders got thoroughly beaten by Portland 3-1 and then recorded only one shot against Sporting Kansas City.

They soon put in Brian Schmetzer as interim coach. Not a problem, right? Interim coaches don't just salvage a season out of the blue and win trophies... Never happens.

As the season approached the final stretch, I had recognized the situation that Sounders were in. They were just below the line. They had a tough stretch of games, which included having to play LA on the road. Going into the LA game, I remember talking to a colleague about the upcoming battle. He wasn't too optimistic about it stating they hadn't won in LA since 2009. Then I reminded him and half-heartedly said, "Well, you guys had Sigi all those years. Now it's someone new."

I don't really consider myself superstitious by any means. However, I have this belief that if you tell people they have a chance, then the opposite will happen because the universe has nothing better to do than make me look a schmuck. Like some sort of "reverse luck." In this case, I wanted them to lose horribly. I mean, there was no way that they were going to beat the Galaxy at StubHub Center, right? Especially with a new coach on board.

Seattle scored four goals. In Los Angeles. Against the Galaxy. And win 4-2. That's not suppose to happen. What on earth is going on?

That game was part of a four game winning streak for Sounders. How was this happening? They have an interim coach. They've come back from their really terrible start to compete for a playoff spot. Timbers are struggling, particularly on the road. I tried to soothe myself thinking that everything was going to be fine....

Everything is going to be fine, Ed... Everything is going to be fine....

Like that.

My coed rec soccer team had won a tournament over the summer and the prize was suite tickets to Sounders game against Real Salt Lake. Of all the games we got, it was Decision Day. Thankfully, there were multiple televisions in our suite so I could keep track of the Timbers game in addition to watching Sounders game. Sounders needed to win. Timbers needed to beat Vancouver. So many games mattered that day that emotions were going to be all over the place depending on the outcomes.

Decision Day started off with chaos. Goals were getting scored by every team-except mine. To further add to that, I looked up on the screen and saw Vancouver get the opening goal. At this point the Timbers would miss playoffs and Sounders would be in. However, it was only thirteen minutes into the game, so there was a chance for a comeback.

Everything is going to be fine, Ed... Everything is going to be fine....

Sounders retook the lead again with Roldan's goal. Then Vancouver get two more goals. Sounders are winning 2-1. I'm just thinking to this Portland team:

"You're killing me Smalls." Smalls didn't know what s'mores were. Timbers didn't know this was going to be the end of their season.

This is how the season is going to end. Not with a bang, but with a complete slaughtering.

At full time, everyone's hugging each other in the suite because they know that Sounders made it to the playoffs for the a millionth time running. Vancouver nailed the coffin shut on the Timbers' season by scoring one more goal to give them four on the day. Not even Valeri's penalty could make me feel better. Not only that, but Vancouver got to hoist Cascadia Cup as well.

I just stood there looking at the screen in complete dismay. A buddy of mine that's a Sounders fan stands next to me, puts a hand on my shoulder, and says "It's alright, dude."

Well, Timbers can't defend the Cup. That's alright. I mean, there's no way that Sounders will have a chance, right?

"Everything is going to be fine, Ed, isn't it?"

A colleague and I were talking about Sounders' changes and this seemed very familiar to both of us. Timbers did very much the same thing in pulling off a superb run at the very end of the season. So even though I was hoping it couldn't happen, I knew that anything was possible. The parallels were unavoidable.

2016 seemed to be the year of the underdogs.

Portugal beat favorites and hosts France in France in Euro 2016. Leicester City won the EPL. Cleveland Cavaliers came back from a 3-1 deficit to beat the Golden State Warriors. Chicago Cubs themselves come back from a 3-1 deficit to beat all odds against the Cleveland Indians to win their first World Series since 1908. And somehow in the United States, in the presidential election... Well, you guys all know how that went.

The first round match for Sounders was against Sporting Kansas City. After having seen Kansas City get beaten by the double posts against Portland, I thought they'd come hard and redeem themselves from last year's heartbreak. But the luck that evaded them in 2015, evaded them even further when three key refereeing decisions all went against them, and they fell 1-0.

Sounders' next round opponents were FC Dallas. Despite not having Mauro Diaz due to a season-ending Achilles injury, this Dallas team was young and talented. They were the season's Supporter Shield winners after all and many people's favourites for the trophy.

Seattle scores three goals in a span of 10 minutes to give them a 3-0 lead at home off a Lodeiro brace. Then the new Sounders playmaker kills off the game with a crucial away goal. Sounders advance to the Western Conference finals. Thanks Dallas. Of all the days to take a quick siesta.

There's this little comic that exists.

It features a dog with a hat, sitting in a house that's burning down. And there's a cup of coffee on the table. He's just sitting there and saying, "This is fine."

I feel like this is what I'm telling myself right now. Sounders have always seemed to fall short in playoffs though. They hadn't made it to the MLS Cup before. Colorado was looking pretty decent, particularly defensively. Surely, they would end Seattle's run. And altitude and Jermaine Jones and...and....

Next thing I know, Seattle over two legs to make it to the MLS Cup and I am numb with disbelief if such a thing is possible.

It was Toronto versus Seattle. Leading up to that MLS Cup Final, a bunch of our friends in the Timbers group were talking about the game in our group page on Facebook.

Then after thinking about all the things happening in 2016 with comebacks, I posted this with such pain, agony, and regret:

"Given how 2016 and it's the year of the underdogs, Sounders will probably win this...."

I was kind of hoping that this would give me some reverse luck and that Sounders would lose because of it. Toronto had, after all, looked really throughout the playoffs, scoring seventeen goals and only conceding six over five games. They had Michael Bradley, Jozy Altidore, and one of the best players in the league in Sebastian Giovinco. It's Toronto's game to lose.

I'd become that dog.

Everything is going to be alright. Everything is going to be alright... Dog in a house that's burning down, drinking his coffee.

I tried not to watch the game. In the slim case that Sounders did win, I didn't want to see them hoist the cup live on the feed. But it was impossible for me to not to push that red button and see what happens. I pull up the game in the second half and start watching. Part of me is laughing through the game because of the hilarity that came from it. Toronto couldn't score for the life of them. Sounders looked like they were absolutely miles behind Toronto in terms of play.

Then Frei's save happened. I'm guessing that moment is written about somewhere else in this book. Probably in every chapter.

I just couldn't believe it. It was like he took a chopping axe and swung it right into my heart. Not just once. With every replay of

it, it was like he did it again... and again... and again. I knew at that point there was no way that Toronto was going to win this match. Sounders were destined to win this. Surely, enough the game goes to penalties and Roman Torres kills a part of me by hitting the game-winning penalty that secure them the Cup.

My hand were on my face just thinking, "I can't believe this is happening... They won the Cup."

I slouched in my chair a bit, as I was somewhat in shock. No longer could we as Timbers fans say, "We have a star and you don't."

Because they somehow defied all odds and continued on the trend of 2016 being the year of the underdogs and winning the MLS Cup. I'd meet up with some teammates from that rec soccer team over drinks and they'd remind me of how Sounders won the cup. "Well, you know what? Sounders are MLS Cup champs now!"

I'm never trusting reverse luck or dogs in burning houses ever again.

Chapter Sixteen

Travel Tales
3 ECS Members Tell Their Stories

By Martin Corpus, Tom Sewell and Tal Levy

Martin Corpus started watching Sounders in 2005 and plays for ECS FC. Tom Sewell is a Cambridge United fan. Tal Levy is a Seattle native USC grad and SoCal Sound member.

Never letting go of that Champions feeling

By Martin Corpus

I remember I had just gotten off the bus in Finn Hill in the middle of a rainy November evening. I was stressed because my professor at UW Bothell had practically totaled my project for being too contrived. Hustling my ass home, I was saying, "come on Montreal," to myself a million times in the hopes of a home final in Seattle. When the Eastern Conference match ended, my jaw was dropped and glued to the floor. I couldn't believe my Sounders had to go to Toronto for the MLS Cup.

Two after plans were set in stone, my dad slowly drove to SEATAC Airport and the adventure began with a redeye flight. I ran into Esco Strong and his wife who were on the same flights as me. When we got to Toronto, he gave me an impromptu history lesson about the city's commercial buildings and how Toronto is sometimes used as a 'fake NYC' in movies.

After we left the airport, I met up with Brian and Megan Walker. We went to Steam Whistle Brewing for some beer sampling, toured

a small park with some old shutdown trains and tracks, and then proceeded to our rented townhouse on the edge of town. The kitchen was big enough for us three to sit down for some tea and goldfish crackers.

At a bar called The Loose Moose, there was a whole underground floor reserved just for ECS that night. So many members from all over the world had traveled for what was bound to be the most unforgettable awayday ever. I saw people from every subgroup and met some new faces as well (including Cristian Roldan's parents). My heart was warm, my soul drunk with happiness. It was like being part of an MC where every chapter had one massive meetup. There was nothing more beautiful than seeing almost every member of "Brougham Faithful" packed into one place.

The day of the match finally came and my eyes popped open faster than a champagne cork. I put on my signature black vest, then a giant coat the size of myself, and walked out of the town house. I was tasked, with yet another friend of mine, to scope out a good marching route. When we did, we found ourselves on the opposite side of the train platform from the rest of the group. We brought back the chant "Everywhere We Go" which transitioned

Sounders Fans on form in San Jose
Photo by Lyndsay Radnedge

to "Duwamish Sown" until the train arrived. We drowned out the singing locals and rolled on to BMO Field.

Once everyone made it to their seats, I had no idea where to sit! Andres Gallegos was kind enough to invite me to stand with him and the ECS originals in the back of the crowd. The match started, I was freezing my ass off, and without realizing it, I was holding on to my friend Roby Branom for dear life for the duration of the whole 120-minute match.

When extra time kicked off, I was still holding on to Robby and asked him, "Why the hell are we doing this?" To which he replied, "Because this is awesome!"

How we managed to hold out for penalties is something I'll never figure out. When I saw Brad Evans score after Altidore to keep the shootout level, I had a feeling we could still win it all. Then came Stefan Frei's lone save of the shootout and a rise in hope.

After Flaco Fernandez's miss was reconciled by Joevin Jones scoring, I almost fainted. Justin Morrow ran up for shot two kicks later and smacked it OFF THE BAR. I wanted to flail my arms like Stewie Griffin. Roman Torres stood at the spot next then stepped back for a short run up. He gave it the ol' "screw it, this ends now" kind of kick that was swift and wrong-footed Clint Irwin and that was it: Champions of MLS. I took in a moment I would never forget. When Ozzie Alonso raised the trophy, I shed just as many tears as the next bloke then made my way out of the stadium.

What followed after was a series of naps on random floors, Subway sandwiches, a video with Brad Evans to thank my parents for meeting me halfway to fund the trip, and goofing off during a Minneapolis layover with Peter Cho. I made the safe trip back to Seattle and couldn't stop smiling for the entire next day in school. I ditched class the Tuesday after Sounders won the Cup to complete the journey with the champions' parade. I was lucky enough to lead

"Everywhere We Go" again, this time with an ECS Co-founder and my capo mentor. It was without a doubt a part of my senior year highlight reel. College wouldn't have been complete without it.

It really does take a Sounder to raise a trophy, a family of supporters to make football possible, and a fire to be fed to keep passion alive. The 2016 MLS Cup was a journey I'll pass on to my nieces and nephews, future generations of the ECS, and my future students when I become a college-level teacher in about 10 to 12 years from now. Until then, I'll just smile and remember the journey and never let go of that champions feeling.

A whole new meaning to the U District

By Tom Sewell

My Sounders love affair started on a Tuesday night in April 2008 behind a computer, in England. My team, Cambridge United (known as the U's) had just qualified for the promotion playoffs for the first time since our relegation from the professional league structure 3 years earlier,, and knowing one of our major shareholders, Adrian Hanauer, was owner of Sounders, I decided to seek out fans of our "sister" club. Having eventually stumbled onto the forum of the ECS, not knowing what on earth that acronym stood for, I shared our story and its background, explained our connections, and left expecting nothing more.

I got responses, with interest in us shown, and started to dig into this mysterious American team further. At this point in my life I took a stereotypical English view of American soccer, looked down on them as if they knew no better, but what I found astonished me and changed my life forever. Before I knew it, I was up at 3am on a weekly basis watching this second division outfit, discussing and learning with these Sounders fans who at that time were the heart of the club. I grew to know Le Toux, Graham, Levesque, Eylander,

I cheered as Sounders took scalp after scalp in the US Open Cup, usually as the sun was coming up, I learnt what a local derby that's 200 miles away could be all about, and I found myself wanting more.

Alas, at this time I was only 18, and so I pursued through the first two seasons of the MLS Sounders in the same vein that I had previously, but friendships had grown, I had met one of the ECS founders in Europe, I had taken another member to a Cambridge game, and by the time the 2011 season, and 21, had come around, it was time for me to get my first live taste of Seattle the team and Seattle the place.

Fuel, McCoys, Temple, the March to the March, the Brougham End, all became a reality on a Saturday afternoon in June 2011, names became faces, I could finally belt out the ECS songbook rather than hum it quietly so as not to wake my housemates, and I was blown away by it all. Seattle wasn't going to be a one off, this was where I want to be, these are the people I want to be with, this was now my city.

I've visited Seattle a further 9 times since that first trip, I rarely have to introduce myself in the Brougham End anymore, I don't need a map, I don't need a tourist guide, Seattle is my home-from-home, and Sounders are an embedded part of that. I've followed the team to Chicago, I've capoed in New York, I've lived and breathed the derby in Portland, I've had an experience I will never forget in a US Open Cup game in San Francisco, and it all feels as natural to me in green and blue as it does when I don the amber and black of Cambridge.

I have been fortunate to share my city and my team with a significant number of Sounders too, to be able to replicate the hospitality I have received from so many, and whilst Sounders have now usurped Cambridge United in size compared to the USL days, in the stands I like to think there are still a considerable number of us who have kept that partnership going.

Time moves on, people grow up, and frequently watching games at 3 in the morning is no longer an option, my viewership of Sounders has changed not only with age, but with the experiences I've had in Seattle and across America, because TV just doesn't cut it anymore compared to the real thing, although I will still always watch those pesky early kick offs which are rather convenient for an Englishman.

But, of course, I made the effort for that night in Toronto, having come back from Cambridge's furthest away trip of our season (incidentally, as far as Portland is from Seattle), stumbling in 5 minutes before kick off, and suffering through the next two hours like the rest of Seattle before that unbridled moment of joy and relief when the final spot kick went in. I was happy I saw it, I was happy for the team, but most of all I was happy for everyone who had welcomed me into their surroundings for the eight years prior, the many people I now call friends, and fellow Sounders.

5,000 miles may separate us, but the last nine years mean I can call Seattle home, bleed blue and green, and consider myself a Sounder.

Souders here, Sounders there, Sounders every...where

By Tal Levy

I landed in Toronto at 7am local time the day of MLS Cup. Despite having under two weeks between the Eastern Conference Finals and the match, I and three Seattle expats – living in Berkeley, Los Angeles, and Boston had secured flights and hotels, knowing that Sounders' first MLS Cup was an away trip we couldn't miss. The camaraderie had already begun the night before when a man saluted me with his Sounders scarf as I walked through the LAX security line, but when we stepped out onto the streets of downtown Toronto later that morning, I was seeing Sounders fans everywhere. At least once per block, I spotted a rave green jacket, hat, or scarf.

After a quick nap, my group grabbed lunch and picked up our tickets from the ECS hotel – and caught a grinning Roman Torres taking pictures with fans in the hotel lobby. As the day wore on, we headed to the ECS pre-funk bar, the streets were filled with packs of roving Sounders fans. It was my first time walking the streets of Toronto and the downtown felt more like downtown Seattle on a matchday than a city in a foreign country.

When we got into the bar, it was completely packed. Another friend had managed to snag a table (but no seats), so eight of us huddled around a bar table meant for two. To make the crowding more complicated, everybody in the bar had been heavily bundled up for the near-freezing outside temperatures, and had shed several layers in the heated indoor bar. Although the bar had upped their staffing for the day, they were far from prepared for an ECS crowd – drinks and food took a long time to get to us, and by an hour before we left nearly all of the bar's kegs were tapped out. Several supporters decided to forgo the atmosphere in favor of timely drinks by heading to the nearby bar.

For me, however, the atmosphere more than made up for the overcrowding and overworked service. The entire bar was filled with a nervous energy. Just months before, Sounders had looked like they were going to miss the playoffs entirely, and now that we were here, it was still a little tough to believe. Every conversation quickly turned to some iteration on "what's going to happen tonight?" At other away days – Vancouver, Portland, Los Angeles, San Jose, Kansas City – the energy has always tended closer to a celebratory atmosphere. Here, every supporter (myself included) was too nervous to drink much, too focused on being fully present for the match.

Finally, it became time for us to head to the stadium. We donned our jackets, opened up our hand-warmers, and trekked down to Union Station. A handful of confused locals watched and listened as each car filled up with singing, scarf-swinging Sounders fans. In BMO Field, much of the pregame passed in a blur – the only festivities I really remember were the two tifos. As usual with ECS tifo, we helped hold it up and then consulted with our neighbors and Twitter to find out what it said – "Win Tonight, Live Forever". A perfectly simple message that expressed why I was here, having traveled across the continent for the opportunity to witness my club at the most historic moment of its MLS history.

The game begun in earnest, and as usual ECS began singing. Compared to home games, when ECS sections are usually primarily concerned with full-participation in the ECS songs and chants, away games can often be a bit scattered, especially with fans unused to following capos. In Toronto, we had a different problem: at each dangerous breakaway, the crowd would falter out of pure excitement or nervous energy. This happened a lot, with Toronto FC largely dominating possession through regulation. Each time a nervous moment ended, the capos would bring the crowd back into song as strong as ever, urging our Sounders to keep playing, to keep fighting.

When extra time was called, I had to sit down. The pit in my stomach was overwhelming, and all I could remember was the last time I had attended an away Cup Final – in Kansas City when our quest for a fourth Open Cup was hampered by a call against Michael Gspurning for leaving his line during the shootout. Somehow, I was sure that some equally-horrific miscarriage of justice was going to happen.

But it didn't. Roman Torres blasted a perfect penalty to win the shootout, and the section erupted in jubilation. I was crying, leaping up and down, hugging everybody I could reach. We stayed in the stadium and pushed as close as we could to the field, saluting and

Sounders FC at MLS Cup
Photo by Max Aquino

cheering every Sounder as they raised the cup. Only when the team had left the field did we make our way out, to celebrate with the rest of ECS in downtown Toronto, to soak up the moment and have the perfect matchday last forever.

pg 134: The Three Amigos

pg 135: Bodysurfing
Photos by Max Aquino

Chapter Seventeen

Toronto Rattle in the Goals
How the East Was Won

By Steve Clare

Steve Clare is the founder of Prost Amerika and Prost Publishing.

TFC ring Philadelphia's bell and hit baseball score at Yankee Stadium

Over in the Eastern Conference, results were not exactly being ground out as they were in the West. 8 playoff games produced 33 goals, compared to just 17 in the Western Conference. On average, you'd see two goals a game more watching an EC playoff game. Toronto scored 17 of those 33, meaning that they matched the entire goal tally of the WC in playoff goals.

The 'Red Machine' had put three past Philadelphia in the same round as Sounders had beaten SKC. Amazingly, that became seven in the home and home series with NYCFC. They took a reasonable 2-0 lead at home to visit New York, and followed that up with a humiliating 5-0 thumping of NYCFC at Yankee Stadium.

The extent of that humiliation bears some repeating. The away goal that took the tie out of NYCFC's reach took just six minutes. By half-time, it was 3-0 and by full time 5-0. Very expensive foreign signings Frank Lampard and David Villa played the full 90 minutes. On the comments sections of the internet sites, there was general jubilation across both countries. It was as if the league had united

behind Toronto to exact revenge on the MLS hierarchy for the favors seemingly done to get NYC into MLS before they had a stadium. Cynicism about Lampard's commitment to the league wasn't even just confined to fans of other clubs.

For many, at least outside Vancouver and Montreal, Toronto represented many of the good things about MLS. Their long suffering fanbase had stayed with them through years of underachievement. They were among the first in MLS to develop a vibrant Supporter Culture. They are credited with bringing large away travel to the league following an epic match in Columbus in 2008. They were, in simplistic terms, authentic – everything which NYCFC were not to many diehards.

In short, it was easy to revel in the light blues misery, and only a few diehards could not help but be pleased for Toronto, especially as, in Michael Bradley and Jozy Altidore, they relied on American skills at the top not European. Toronto didn't have any reason to care how others vicariously reveled in their triumph, but nonetheless the result reverberated across MLS. "Firing on all cylinders" didn't even begin to describe the level that Bradley, Altidore and Sebastian Giovinco had reached. While storylines in the west

Toronto celebrate their Conference Championship
Photo by Nick Turchiaro/ USA TODAY Sports Images

focused on Sounders' all-important appearance in the big game, top nationwide analysts spoke mostly of the Toronto juggernaut – could anyone stop them, once they started running downhill?

The next in line to try and stop them had more motivation than any other club

The rivals of all rivals settle all Canadian final

After a victory that perhaps united all fans, came a match that strictly divided Canada.

The Eastern Conference match-up was that ultimate derby; Ontario v Quebec, Anglophone v Francophone, Toronto v Montreal showdown. The two clubs were in addition two old USL rivals. It was a real rivalry with real history and a far cry from the perceived artificiality of NYCFC. Their derby is one of the biggest in the league, and probably the closest east coast equivalent to the Seattle-Portland rivalry, except it also has politics and language, and is predated by a lot longer history.

You could probably write a book by itself on the 210 breathless minutes that the two Canadian clubs put on show for their own country and the USA. Yes, Toronto scored seven goals over the two legs just as they had versus New York. Yes, they had scored five in the second leg just as they has at Yankee Stadium.

But that's where the similarities ended.

Montreal Impact held a 3-2 lead after the first leg. The story was more that they had blown a 3-0 lead and allowed TFC to edge back into the contest.

It had looked like doom for Toronto coach Greg Vanney at 3-0 down. Dominic Oduro, Matteo Mancosu and Ambroise Oyongo had steered the Quebecers into a 53rd minute dreamland. However

the late goals for the visitors from the American duo of Altidore and Bradley had radically altered the slant of the tie. How could Montreal possibly keep a clean sheet at BMO Field in the return leg? The Reds weren't just beating their playoff opponents. They had been throttling them.12 playoff goals had flowed from just four matches in what was the most impressive postseason attacking performance in league history.

The Western Conference champions hoped the Impact might be able to. If they could, Seattle would host MLS Cup. While Toronto's regular season dwarfed Sounders' mark, Montreal had slipped into the playoffs with three fewer points than Seattle did. As such the second leg was received with an abundance of caution and excitement in Seattle.

When Dominic Oduro put Montreal 4-2 up on aggregate on 25 minutes, the dream scenario of a final in Seattle seemed to be on. That dissipated before half time as Armando Cooper and the superb Altidore netted to put Toronto ahead on away goals as the juggernaut kicked into gear. After the break Montreal again tossed a wrench in the works. Star Ignacio Piatti's 53rd minute goal levelled the match at 2-2 on the night and had the Impact ahead once more. A Nick Hagglund goal however sent the match to extra time at 3-2.

Toronto managed two unanswered in the additional thirty minutes from Benoit Cheyrou and Tosaint Ricketts to ensure a 7-5 win on aggregate. Once again they had scored seven goals in a two leg series, and five goals again in a second leg. Lastly, they had guaranteed home advantage for the MLS Cup Final. Toronto hadn't just advanced, they'd matched their own berserk performance in the Big Apple. One historic playoff thrashing was impressive, two in several weeks was dominant. It seemed like an eternity since they had been 3-0 down in Montreal.

With Toronto joining Seattle in the final, MLS was set for its first ever final between two expansion clubs; franchises who had not been there at the start.

As soon as the dust settled, more than a thousand Sounders supporters made plans for their trek out to Toronto. Passports were located at the bottom of sock drawers. Plane tickets sold out quickly. Hotel rooms were nabbed and demand for a seat in the tiny away allocation at BMO Field was frantic. For those around the club, it seemed like just about everyone was trying to find a way to reach the historic match.

pg 140: Torono fans watch the final apprehensively
Photo by Matt Warso

pg 141: Toronto scored as many playoff goals as the West
Photo by John E. Sokolowsi/ USA TODAY Sports Images

Chapter Eighteen

The Final Sounders Roar

By Steven Agen

Steven Agen is the Seattle Editor for Prost Amerika and founder of Radio Cascadia.

Pregame Buildup

The coverage leading up to MLS Cup focused on the two biggest unknowns in the match – the weather, and the injury situation. It was no secret that Toronto, as both the home side and the goal-scoring behemoth, were prohibitive favorites against the banged up visitors. Sounders' impressive control performances in the playoffs would matter for little if they couldn't keep the Reds off the scoreboard. All Toronto had to do was replicate the attacking success of their previous five outings and the 17 goals they scored, one more time.

As Sounders fans streamed into Toronto in the week before the Saturday match they could see why the weather commanded the attention it did. Icy temperatures and frequent snow storms ripped through Ontario on Thursday and Friday, inciting questions about whether the final would affected or even able to go ahead if such conditions continued. Conventional wisdom held that Seattle would benefit more from a weather-impact match than the Reds – snow games are fluky games. It was tough to construct another game state that brought Sounders to even close to a 50-50 shot at winning, barring a penalty shootout of course. Maybe a frozen field

and bitter cold would put a damper on the hottest attack the MLS postseason had ever witnessed.

The other big piece of news surrounded high profile injuries on each side of the equation. Neither club could have faced a more debilitating absence than those hanging over them. Osvaldo Alonso was diagnosed with a sprained knee following the Colorado series, while Sebastian Giovinco also had to sub off in the second leg of his Conference Championship. No one outside the clubs new if either player would be able to start in the final.

The health of Jordan Morris was a concern for Sounders as well. After injuring himself while scoring the only goal at Colorado in the previous round, Morris had insisted he stay on the field and completed the ninety minutes. Seattle had needed all of their substitutions on the night and Morris' grit was a saving grace, but at what cost in the final?

The History

Sounders' all-time record against Toronto was perhaps the most encouraging statistic pointing in their favor. Eleven MLS meetings

had produced seven wins for Seattle and two more draws along with it. Of Toronto's two wins over Sounders, only one came at BMO Field where Seattle had recorded prior three victories. Home or away, long ago or lately, Sounders were used to positive results against Toronto FC.

The most recent match between the two was 1-1 draw in Ontario on July 2nd, almost exactly a month before Seattle's turnaround started. The Reds were without both Jozy Altidore and Michael Bradley that day, but Nicolas Lodeiro hadn't joined up with Seattle yet either. The summer fixture marked the only regular season meeting between the clubs in 2016. Including playoff matches Toronto posted a home record of 11-6-3 while Sounders' 2016 road mark stood at 5-4-10. By the time December had rolled around, the 1-1 draw in July seemed a distant memory and hardly indicative of what MLS Cup would hold.

BMO Field itself would hold extra fans on the day, expanded to a 36,000 person capacity from its normal 30,000. The change was made for the Grey Cup several weeks prior and large temporary grandstands in the home supporters end stayed through MLS Cup. Toronto's home is large to begin with by MLS standards – the additional seating made it even more imposing. The way that stadium staff had wheeled in extra bleachers in the parking lot behind one endzone gave the impression of trying to fit everybody possible within it. In the same vein as Jurgen Klopp's "Fortress Anfield," it truly felt like Cup Final BMO Field. Seattle fans managed to get their hands on about a thousand tickets, with most tucked away together in a corner of the upper deck.

As fans filed in early for the 8pm kickoff the most immediately apparent interest among them was still the weather. While snow was predicted for Sunday and Monday as it had fallen on Thursday and Friday, MLS Cup Saturday saw little precipitation fall. It have just been too cold for it. At kickoff the temperature was a frigid 23 degrees Fahrenheit. Sporting Kansas City and Real Salt Lake

contested the 2013 edition of the final in colder conditions yet but no other previous MLS Cup could match it for extreme weather.

Erik Friberg came back into the starting eleven for Andreas Ivanschitz, providing more of a third box to box midfielder in the formation rather than the Austrian's more attack-based contributions. The Swede was Schmetzer's only change from their success in Colorado with both Jordan Morris and Osvaldo Alonso cleared to start and play through their pain.

Giovinco made the starting eleven for Greg Vanney and the Reds also went nearly unchanged from their 5-2 romp over Montreal. Jonathan Osorio took Will Johnson's place in midfield but no other switches were made. All awaited visual confirmation that both Toronto's Atomic Ant and Sounders' bullish captain were actually able to play, but otherwise the starting lineups for the match were just as those on the outside expected.

The atmosphere was vibrant as warmups began. The league had been doing its best to emphasize away travel for MLS Cup ever since it switched to the higher-seed-hosts format, and this matchup was a dream come true from that perspective. Toronto had long held the title of best supported club in the Eastern Conference while Sounders had travelled as well as anyone since joining MLS. Both were at their very most vocal in their clubs' biggest hour.

After lengthy and ceremonious pregame festivities, the giant bust of the Philip F. Anschutz Trophy was carted off the field and the players took their places. Center referee Alan Kelly blew his whistle and the 21st edition of MLS Cup was underway.

The match kicked off to immediate and relentless Toronto FC pressure. The hosts looked serious about continuing their fine playoff form early and often – Giovinco chested down for Altidore whose deflected shot went just wide from inside the area before even 120 seconds had elapsed. Alonso cleared the resulting corner but Sounders looked like they were really in for a long night after Frei had to parry another Bradley corner off the goalline on the stroke of four minutes. The Reds had scored three times on only four corners in the Eastern Conference Championship second leg against Montreal – giving up frequent early set pieces seemed a lethal proposition for Seattle.

Sounders grew into the game after the shaky opening five minutes, with Clint Irwin hauling in several crosses from Seattle fullbacks. None were terribly threatening but reaching the final third was an improvement on the opening exchanges.

Osorio forced Frei into a save low to his left with a shot through traffic and the tidal wave of TFC harassment continued through the quarter hour. By the time Giovinco's free kick from a good position on 32 minutes struck the Seattle wall, his hot start with Altidore had faded. He was still lively but signs were there that Toronto's highest paid player and the league's most creative influence wasn't even close to 100% fitness.

Alonso was fortunate to not see a card for a hard challenge on Giovinco six minutes later. The Italian again put his free kick from a useful spot into the Seattle wall. Sounders ended the half with their best chance so far, with Joevin Jones' cut back towards Alonso in the area missing the mark.

Half-time — Toronto FC 0 : 0 Sounders FC

Seattle made it to the break on level terms, and that was the best they had going for them. Half chances mentioned prior were just that, and no clear path to goal seemed evident with TFC keeping a tight lockdown on Lodeiro. The Reds, for their part, controlled the vast majority of the play without exhibiting any real inspiration. From half-time it already was clear that Sounders' best chance was making it to a shootout, unless perhaps a freak snow storm were to hit.

Toronto continued to press for an opening goal after the restart. Giovinco put his best chance of the night wide of the near right hand post on 49' but with most of a half to play Sounders weren't close to out of the woods. Cristian Roldan got in the way of Armando Cooper's strike from distance on 55 minutes, deflecting out for a corner and away from a crowded penalty area as their defending began to take on a desperate if not heroic quality.

Marshall shielded Altidore away from a low cross in the goal area in the 66th minute; Seattle were sitting in as deep as ever, but Toronto's lack of inspiration became more manifest the longer the match stayed scoreless. For the first hour it seemed a question of when and not if Toronto would score. As Giovinco's final product continued to lack the quality needed to beat Frei, a Toronto goal didn't seem like such a certainty anymore. He just didn't look like he had anything in the tank – at least not compared to Alonso, who

kept on in his workmanlike style through the pain of his sprained knee. Giovinco wasn't going to be able to deliver the Cup himself; while Sounders looked no closer to scoring (they finished the half without a shot), Toronto's sudden lack of attacking ideas left a clear path to victory for them. It'd just take 120 minutes to accomplish.

Toronto's MLS Cup tifo
Photo by Matt Warso

Alvaro Fernandez subbed on for Erik Friberg a moment later with Seattle's first change. Andreas Ivanschitz would follow seven minutes after that when he replaced Nelson Valdez, pushing Morris up top in the process.

Will Johnson and Benoit Cheyrou replaced Osorio and Cooper in the last fifteen minutes of regular time, a period characterized by the most frenetic and open sequences of the match so far. The match was stretched with few clear opportunities until Toronto earned another corner halfway through three added minutes. Frei pawed Johnson's header off of Bradley's service away from Altidore, just beating the forward to the ball on the far post. The Seattle goalkeeper took a shot from Altidore for his troubles following the clearance, but most importantly Sounders had made it to extra time. Sounders' 3 total shots through 90 minutes had yielded an exceptionally improved result in the cold in Toronto compared to the heat of Kansas City.

Extra Time and Penalties

Cheyrou had Frei beaten with a low shot from distance a mere 20 seconds into extra time but the effort rolled just wide of the post. He followed up with another strike from outside the box four minutes later but this time Frei was equal to it. All of extra time would to belong to him, soon enough.

A goal would have been the best cure for the angst of the Seattle faithful, but seeing Giovinco limp off with Toronto's last substitution soon after the chance was a close second. The most pedigreed player on the field wasn't going to be able to fake another fifteen minutes in order to take a penalty. Sounders felt a huge step closer to reaching their goal when Tosaint Ricketts replaced him on 103 minutes.

Seattle began the second period of extra time with a Morris cross that Fernandez nearly reached. Evans subbed on for Jordan Morris. Then Frei stole the show.

Only on the field for four minutes, Ricketts reached a ball on the right endline and chipped a cross back for Jozy Altidore in the center of the box. Altidore leapt high into the air, out jumping everyone around him before looping a header over Frei and towards the right post. Sounders' goalkeeper made some fine stops in the 2016 postseason, but the one on 108 minutes in MLS Cup transcended the year and instantly became the most iconic save in the match's history.

Frei stared the ball down and pushed off his left foot to dive at it. The effort seemed to be a formality on first sight. He was just too far from the ball to be able to make a play on it. If Jozy Altidore tried that header another thousand times, he couldn't have placed it any better than he did that night. It was truly the perfect redirection and the BMO Field crowd prepared for celebration.

As Frei pushed Altidore's shot off the line, the roar of the crowd was the loudest of the night. Their support turned into one collective groan – how was Toronto going to get a better look than that? They weren't. Sounders saw the last twelve minutes out and Alan Kelly blew his whistle to bring extra time to a close.

Full time and on to penalties — Toronto FC 0 : 0 Sounders FC

Making it to penalties felt like one hell of an accomplishment. Zero shots in the first half, three in the second, and none in extra time had been coupled with the defensive work of a lifetime. Whereas Giovinco subbed off before match's end, Alonso had written himself into MLS Cup lore. Seattle's captain required four knee injections before the game and four more at half-time to gut it through all 120 minutes. After five Open Cup Final appearances with Seattle and one more with Charleston Battery, Alonso wasn't going to let his knee sprain deter him from completing his club's first ever MLS Cup.

The accomplishment brought with it a better chance at winning than any other opportunity they could have set themselves up with – to be honest, Sounders were never even close to a 50/50 of winning the match outright. Toronto won the right to begin the shootout and the statistical advantage that goes with it but getting there gave Sounders a new lease on life regardless.

Sounders' last shootout was in the Open Cup in June, but featured Tyler Miller in goal rather than Stefan Frei. Frei's last spotkick showdown was in Frisco the previous November as Sounders were eliminated from the 2015 postseason. There were no doubts about Frei's confidence now, having just made The Save while Clint Irwin had mostly just watched proceedings for the last two hours. Between the parallels with the Dallas match in 2015 and the Sporting KC one in July, Sounders suddenly had the chance to put several nightmares to bed in addition to winning a first MLS Cup.

Jozy Altidore and Brad Evans each converted their penalties for 1-1 after one round.

Michael Bradley stepped up next and hit a weak penalty towards the bottom right corner. Frei read it all the way, and Sounders had the advantage in the shootout. For the first time all night the Seattle away contingent truly came to life. Andreas Ivanschitz confidently made it 2-1 and Toronto were really starting to rue all of the missed opportunities throughout the match.

The pendulum of momentum swung back the other way quickly. Cheyrou opened round three by scoring for the Reds and then Alvaro Fernandez put his side footed penalty at a perfect height for Irwin to save to his left. 2-2 after three kicks each, all square.

Will Johnson celebrated with extra gusto, perhaps due to local connections and perhaps due to Timbers connections, after he made it 3-2 Toronto. Joevin Jones answered with a left footed penalty into the roof of the net behind the right corner; the Trinidadian was the youngest Sounder entrusted with a penalty and he hit one for the highlight reels.

Drew Moor made it 4-3 Reds with their last attempt, and it seemed fitting when Sounders' season fell squarely on the shoulders of Nicolas Lodeiro. After the diminutive Uruguayan playmaker had won the heart of the city and changed the club's fortunes, the story of 2016 was the story of how far Lodeiro could take Seattle. He converted in nearly the same spot as Jones, and the shootout went on to an extra round.

Morrow miss sparks pandemonium

Justin Morrow smacked the underside of the bar in round six, and Roman Torres stepped up with Seattle's first chance to win MLS Cup. He sent Irwin the wrong way and blasted the ball into the net just to the left of the center of the goal. And just like that, Sounders had done it. After every clearance, every set piece defended, every counter snuffed out it had still always felt like Seattle were trying to pull off a great escape.

In truth every event since Schmetzer had taken over had been a tightrope to walk, from making the playoffs to their various successes in them. It had felt precarious for so long – even when things started to go right, they weren't okay yet. Victories merely delayed what all thought was an inevitable tumble from the tightrope, rather than end goals themselves. But when Torres' penalty went in, all of the nervousness, and stress of such a tight run lifted off Sounders' shoulders.

The players ran over to the corner to celebrate with their delirious followers, and lifted their first MLS Cup moments later.

The dream had come true. It had come true in a fashion few expected. But the truth was laid out in Silver held aloft by men in Rave Green shirts. Sounders were MLS Champions.

Stefan Frei earned MVP honors for his magical performance, and commemorated it with a championship star tattooed on the his left hand that had denied Jozy Altidore in the game's most crucial moment.

All of the club's most vicious traumas were righted in an instant - Sporting KC's 2012 Open Cup title dwarfed, Portland's 2015 MLS Cup upended, Dallas' PK success in Frisco decisively banished from memory and seven years of playoff woes with it - and all after the worst 20 game start in Sounders' MLS history! For a single season to feature both their lowest point ever and their highest seemed as novel as it was unlikely. 2016 turned into the wildest roller coaster ride imaginable, but that made it all the more special now that the trophy had been delivered.

Two days after winning the final, Sounders celebrated with their fans in a downtown parade. The event culminated with a rally at the Seattle Center. Clint Dempsey took the stage and declared, "Now Portland can't say shit!" as the crowd roared its approval. None of Cascadia could. Timbers had bragging rights for nabbing the first

Sounders fans MLS Cup tifo
Photo by Max Aquino

MLS Cup for the region in 2015 but that title only matched the other two for top-flight championships. Not counting myriad Whitecaps Canadian trophies that neither Sounders nor Timbers played for, each club held one all-time first division title dating back to the NASL era: Vancouver won the Soccer Bowl in 1979, Sounders' 1995 A-League title was a top-flight one as MLS did not yet exist, and then Portland's success in 2015. From the historical perspective, Seattle's 2016 MLS Cup title was most significant in that it put them ahead of their local rivals in the most prestigious metric against which the clubs measure each other.

In the heat of the moment the most resonant part of the 2016 triumph was sending Mr. Sounder Zach Scott off into retirement properly. Coupled with Brian Schmetzer's appointment as head coach and Adrian Hanauer's prior move to majority owner, the victory was especially connected to Sounders' heritage. The club's all-time leader in appearances teamed up with the first Seattle head coach to manage him, and they produced a poetic final act. Scott gave his heart and soul for the club, and he did so for years before they enjoyed the popularity of the current era. In that way he embodies the Seattle soccer community, which fostered the environment in which Sounders would eventually excel upon joining MLS.

The trio again proved that Sounders of today stand on the shoulders of giants. The victory closed the chapter on Scott's career, and on Sounders' transition from USL to MLS with it - Scott was the final holdover remaining from the last USL Sounders squad in 2008. The Cup victory was a perfect bookend, both for Zach Scott and for a community that dreamed of this moment since 2007, and had worked to make such a goal attainable for decades before that.

pg 149: Lodeiro and Torres embrace

pg 150: Cup and Confetti
Photos by Denise McCooey

pg 151: Alonso kisses the Cup
Photo by Max Aquino

Contributors & Thanks

Prost Amerika would like to thank the following

WRITERS

Steven Agen, Steve Clare, Martin Corpus, Toby Dunkelberg, Richard Fleming, Andrew Harvey, Tal Levy, Ari Liljenwall, Greg Nickels, Art Thiel, Matt Pentz, Ed Pham and Zach Scott and Tom Sewell.

PHOTOGRAPHERS

Max Aquino, Brandon Bleek, Nick Danielson, Diego Diaz, Corbin Elliott, Graham Green, Mark Hoffman, Denise McCooey, Lyndsay Radnedge, John E. Sokolowsi, Nick Turchiaro, Debby Von Winckelmann and Matt Warso.

SPECIAL THANKS

Alex Caulfield, Jackson Feltz, Ali Gilmore, Radio Cascadia, Matt 'Stretch' Johnson, Meredith Letts, Dan McCooey, Francine Scott, Linda Scott, Sounders FC, Triple Door, USA Today Sports Images and Wade Webber.

Cover photos: Max Aquino, Brandon Bleek, Nick Danielson and Matt Warso

A very special thanks to all of Prost Amerika's beat writers, photographers, readers, supporters and all those who follow Major League Soccer across the globe.

PROSTAMERIKA'S
RESURGENCE

By Steven Agen and the writers, photographers and friends of Prost Amerika

We at Prost would like to thank you for reading our book and hope you enjoyed it.

A project of Prost Amerika, published by Prost Publishing

www.prostamerika.com/books